CST-29 NEW YORK STATE TEACHER CERTIFICATION SERIES

This is your
PASSBOOK for...

Students with Disabilities

Test Preparation Study Guide
Questions & Answers

COPYRIGHT NOTICE

This book is SOLELY intended for, is sold ONLY to, and its use is RESTRICTED to individual, bona fide applicants or candidates who qualify by virtue of having seriously filed applications for appropriate license, certificate, professional and/or promotional advancement, higher school matriculation, scholarship, or other legitimate requirements of education and/or governmental authorities.

This book is NOT intended for use, class instruction, tutoring, training, duplication, copying, reprinting, excerption, or adaptation, etc., by:

1) Other publishers
2) Proprietors and/or Instructors of "Coaching" and/or Preparatory Courses
3) Personnel and/or Training Divisions of commercial, industrial, and governmental organizations
4) Schools, colleges, or universities and/or their departments and staffs, including teachers and other personnel
5) Testing Agencies or Bureaus
6) Study groups which seek by the purchase of a single volume to copy and/or duplicate and/or adapt this material for use by the group as a whole without having purchased individual volumes for each of the members of the group
7) Et al.

Such persons would be in violation of appropriate Federal and State statutes.

PROVISION OF LICENSING AGREEMENTS – Recognized educational, commercial, industrial, and governmental institutions and organizations, and others legitimately engaged in educational pursuits, including training, testing, and measurement activities, may address request for a licensing agreement to the copyright owners, who will determine whether, and under what conditions, including fees and charges, the materials in this book may be used them. In other words, a licensing facility exists for the legitimate use of the material in this book on other than an individual basis. However, it is asseverated and affirmed here that the material in this book CANNOT be used without the receipt of the express permission of such a licensing agreement from the Publishers. Inquiries re licensing should be addressed to the company, attention rights and permissions department.

All rights reserved, including the right of reproduction in whole or in part, in any form or by any means, electronic or mechanical, including photocopying, recording, or by any information storage and retrieval system, without permission in writing from the Publisher.

Copyright © 2025 by
National Learning Corporation

212 Michael Drive, Syosset, NY 11791
(516) 921-8888 • www.passbooks.com
E-mail: info@passbooks.com

PASSBOOK® SERIES

THE *PASSBOOK® SERIES* has been created to prepare applicants and candidates for the ultimate academic battlefield – the examination room.

At some time in our lives, each and every one of us may be required to take an examination – for validation, matriculation, admission, qualification, registration, certification, or licensure.

Based on the assumption that every applicant or candidate has met the basic formal educational standards, has taken the required number of courses, and read the necessary texts, the *PASSBOOK® SERIES* furnishes the one special preparation which may assure passing with confidence, instead of failing with insecurity. Examination questions – together with answers – are furnished as the basic vehicle for study so that the mysteries of the examination and its compounding difficulties may be eliminated or diminished by a sure method.

This book is meant to help you pass your examination provided that you qualify and are serious in your objective.

The entire field is reviewed through the huge store of content information which is succinctly presented through a provocative and challenging approach – the question-and-answer method.

A climate of success is established by furnishing the correct answers at the end of each test.

You soon learn to recognize types of questions, forms of questions, and patterns of questioning. You may even begin to anticipate expected outcomes.

You perceive that many questions are repeated or adapted so that you can gain acute insights, which may enable you to score many sure points.

You learn how to confront new questions, or types of questions, and to attack them confidently and work out the correct answers.

You note objectives and emphases, and recognize pitfalls and dangers, so that you may make positive educational adjustments.

Moreover, you are kept fully informed in relation to new concepts, methods, practices, and directions in the field.

You discover that you are actually taking the examination all the time: you are preparing for the examination by "taking" an examination, not by reading extraneous and/or supererogatory textbooks.

In short, this PASSBOOK®, used directedly, should be an important factor in helping you to pass your test.

NEW YORK STATE TEACHER CERTIFICATION EXAMINATIONS™ INTRODUCTION

GENERAL INFORMATION

About the Testing Program

Those seeking a New York State teaching certificate for the common branch subjects in prekindergarten through grade 6 or for academic subjects in the secondary grades 7 through 12, i.e., English, a language other than English, mathematics, a science (biology, chemistry, earth science, physics), or social studies, must pass the New York State Teacher Certification Examinations (NYSTCE®) as part of the requirements for certification.

Those seeking a New York State teaching certificate in other areas may need to achieve qualifying scores on the NYSTCE® as indicated in the table which follows.

The New York State Teacher Certification Examinations™ program consists of the

- Liberal Arts and Sciences Test (LAST)
- Elementary and Secondary Assessment of Teaching Skills Written (ATS-W)
- Content Specialty Tests (CSTs)
- Language Proficiency Assessments (LPAs)
- Assessment of Teaching Skills - Performance (ATS-P) (Video)

These exams provide an objective basis of competency and skill for teaching in New York State.

For the requirements, check the summary table of testing requirements which follows.

Test Development

The New York State Teacher Certification Examinations™ are criterion referenced and objective based. A criterion-referenced test is designed to measure a candidate's knowledge and skills in relation to an established standard rather than in relation to the performance of other candidates. The purpose of these exams is to certify candidates who have demonstrated requisite knowledge and skills necessary for a public school teacher.

> The New York State Teacher Certification Examination C"NYSTCE.") program was developed and is administered by the New York State Education Department ("NYSED® ") and National Evaluation Systems, Inc. ("NES"), and this test preparation guide was neither developed in connection with these organizations, nor is it endorsed by them. The NES® and NYSTCE®names and logos are registered service marks of. National Evaluation Systems, Inc. for use with testing services and related products.

An individual's performance on a test is evaluated against an established standard. The passing score for each test is established by the New York State Commissioner of Education based on the professional judgments and recommendations of New York State educators. Examinees who do not pass a test may retake it at any of the subsequent scheduled test administrations.

Description of the Tests

The following is a description of the tests within the NYSTCE® program.

Liberal Arts and Sciences Test (LAST). The Liberal Arts and Sciences Test consists of multiple-choice test questions and a written assignment. Candidates are asked to demonstrate conceptual and analytical skills, critical-thinking and communication skills, and multicultural awareness. The test covers scientific and mathematical processes, historical and social scientific awareness, artistic expression and the humanities, communication skills, and written n analysis and expression. The Liberal Arts and Sciences Test is required for a provisional certificate.

Elementary and Secondary Versions of the Assessment of Teaching Skills - Written (ATS-W). There are two versions of the Assessment of Teaching Skills - Written (ATS-W). The elementary ATS-W should be taken by individuals seeking a PreK-6, common branch subject teaching certificate. The secondary ATS-W should be taken by individuals seeking a certificate for a secondary academic subject. Individuals seeking a certificate in other titles may take either the elementary or the secondary ATS-W. The ATS-W is required for a provisional certificate.

The elementary and secondary versions of the Assessment of Teaching Skills - Written consists of multiple-choice test questions and a written assignment. These tests address knowledge of the learner, instructional planning and assessment, instructional delivery, and the professional environment.

Content Specialty Tests (CSTs). There are currently 21 Content Specialty Tests. For a complete list of test titles, see the list that follows.

The Content Specialty Tests (except Japanese, Russian, Mandarin, Cantonese, Hebrew, and Greek) contain multiple-choice test questions. The CSTs for languages other than English also include audiotaped listening and speaking components and writing components. The CSTs are required for a permanent certificate.

Language Proficiency Assessments (ELPA-C, ELPA-N, TLPAs). The Language Proficiency Assessments are required for ESOL certificates and for bilingual education extension certificates in New York State.

Assessment of Teaching Skills - Performance (ATS-P) (video). The Assessment of Teaching Skills - Performance (ATS-P) (video) is one requirement for individuals seeking a permanent New York State teaching certificate in specified areas. For this assessment, candidates are required to prepare a videotape of their instruction with students who are part of their regular teaching assignments in grades PreK through 12. The teaching skills assessed by the ATS-P (video) are defined by the five objectives in the Instructional Delivery subarea of the Assessment of Teaching Skills test framework.

From the official announcement for instructional purposes

TESTS

Test (Test Code)

Liberal Arts and Sciences Test (LAST) (01)
Elementary Assessment of Teaching Skills - Written (ATS-W) (90)
Secondary Assessment of Teaching Skills - Written (ATS-W) (91)
Elementary Education (02)
English (03)
Mathematics (04)
Social Studies (05)
Biology (06)
Chemistry (07)
Earth Science (08)
Physics (09)
Early Childhood (21)
Latin (10)
Cantonese (11)
French (12)
German (13)
Greek (14)
Hebrew (15)
Italian (16)
Japanese (17)
Mandarin (18)
Russian (19)
Spanish (20)
English to Speakers of Other Languages (ESOL) (22)
English Language Proficiency Assessment for Classroom Personnel (ELPA-C) (23)
English Language Proficiency Assessment for Nonclassroom Personnel (ELPA-N) (25)
Target Language Proficiency Assessment - Spanish (24)
Target Language Proficiency Assessment other than Spanish

NEW YORK STATE TEACHER CERTIFICATION TESTING REQUIREMENTS

(Commissioner's Regulation) Teaching Certificates	Current Requirements		Projected Requirements
(8 NYCRR 80.15) PreK-6, Common Branch Subjects	LAST ATS-W CST (Elementary Education) ATS-P	Provisional Provisional Permanent Permanent	Same as current requirements
7-9 Extension	Same as base certificate, PLUS: CST in academic subject	Permanent	Same as current requirements
Early Childhood Annotation (PreK-3)	CST in annotation	Permanent	
(8 NYCRR 80.16) 7-12 Academic Subjects, e.g., English, Language other than English, Mathematics, Science (Biology, Chemistry, Earth Science, Physics), Social Studies	LAST ATS-W CST (in academic subject) ATS-P	Provisional Provisional Permanent Permanent	Same as current requirements
5-6 Extension	Same as base certificate		
(8 NYCRR 80.9) Bilingual Education [Extension]	Same as base certificate, PLUS: LPA in English (oral)* LPA in Target Language (oral & written)*	Prov./Perm. Prov./Perm.	Same as current requirements
(8 NYCRR 80.10) English to speakers of other languages (ESOL)	LAST* ATS-W* LPA in English (oral)* CST* (ESOL) ATS-P*	Provisional Provisional Provisional Permanent Permanent	Same as current requirements
(8 NYCRR 80.5) Occupational Subjects, e.g. Agricultural Subjects, Business/Distributive Education, Health Occupations, Trade Subjects, Technical Subjects, Home Economics Subjects	Baccalaureate-based certificates: LAST + ATS-W or NTE Core Battery Associate & non-degree-based certificate titles: ATS-W or NTE Core Battery	Provisional Permanent	Baccalaureate-based certificates: LAST Provisional ATS-W Provisional CST Permanent ATS-P Permanent Associate & non-degree-based certificate titles: ATS-W Provisional ATS-P Permanent

NEW YORK STATE TEACHER CERTIFICATION TESTING REQUIREMENTS

(Commissioner's Regulation) Teaching Certificates	Current Requirements		Projected Requirements	
(8 NYCRR 80.6) Special Education, e.g. Special Education, Blind/ Partially Sighted, Deaf/ Hearing Impaired Speech/Hearing Handicapped	LAST & ATS-W or NTE Core Battery	Provisional	Same as for PreK-6 or 7-12 certificate, PLUS: Special Education Supplement to ATS-W Special Education supplement to ATS-P	Provisional Permanent
(8 NYCRR 80.7) Reading	LAST & ATS-W or NTE Core Battery	Provisional	Same as for PreK-6 or 7-12 certificate, PLUS: CST in Reading	Permanent
(8 NYCRR 80.8) School Media Specialist	LAST + ATS-W or NTE Core Battery	Provisional	LAST ATS-W CST ATS-P	Provisional Provisional Permanent Permanent
(8 NYCRR 80.17) Special Subjects, e.g. Art, Business/Distributive Education, Dance, Health, Home Economics, Music, Physical Education, Recreation, Speech, Technology Education	LAST + ATS-W or NTE Core Battery	Provisional	LAST ATS-W CST ATS-P	Provisional Provisional Permanent Permanent

LAST = Liberal Arts & Sciences Test
ATS-W = Assessment of Teaching Skills - Written
CST   = Content Specialty Test
ATS-P = Assessment of Teaching Skills - Performance (video)
LPA   = Language Proficiency Assessment

FOR FURTHER INFORMATION

If you have questions regarding which test(s) you must take, contact the teacher certification contact person at your college or:

NEW YORK STATE EDUCATION DEPARTMENT
OFFICE OF TEACHING
CULTURAL EDUCATION CENTER
ALBANY, N.Y. 12230

TELEPHONE: (518) 474-3901
9:00-11:45 A.M., 12:45-4:30 P.M. Eastern Time

Relay center telephone number for the deaf within New York State: 1-800-622-1220

Nationwide AT&T Relay Operator for the Deaf: 1-800-855-2880 (TTY)

If you have questions regarding the Test Registration, Administration Procedures, Admission Ticket, or Score Report, contact:

NYSTCE
NATIONAL EVALUATION SYSTEMS, INC.
30 GATEHOUSE ROAD
P.O. BOX 660
AMHERST, MA 01004-9008

TELEPHONE: (413) 256-2882
9:00 A.M. - 5:00 P.M. Eastern Time

Telephone number for the deaf: (413) 256-8032 (TTY)

Students with Disabilities

About This Test
The Education of Exceptional Students: Mild to Moderate Disabilities test is designed for examinees who plan to teach in a special education program for students with mild to moderate disabilities at any grade level from preschool through grade 12. The constructed-response questions assess the examinee's ability to apply the principles of special education to situations that a teacher is likely to encounter in teaching students with mild to moderate disabilities.
Topics Covered

I. **Assessment**
- Demonstrate knowledge of specialized policies regarding screening, pre-referral strategies, referral, and placement procedures for individuals with mild to moderate disabilities
- Demonstrate knowledge of assessment for eligibility: instruments and methods, both formal and informal (e.g., ecological inventories; portfolio, functional, and assistive-technology assessments) used to determine eligibility for special education services, with consideration given to
    - modality preferences
    - levels of support and/or independence
    - accommodations for test-taking situations
    - cultural and linguistic diversity

- Demonstrate knowledge of assessment for instruction:
    - how to design and adapt assessments, both formal and informal, to use in developing instruction for individuals with mild to moderate disabilities, with consideration given to
        - modality preferences
        - levels of support and/or independence
        - accommodations in test-taking situations
        - cultural and linguistic diversity
    - how to utilize assessment information in developing instruction for individuals with mild to moderate disabilities in both specialized and general-education settings in both
        - academic domains (e.g., mathematics, reading, writing, social studies, science, art, music, vocational) and
        - behavioral domains (e.g., social skills, listening skills, communication skills, self-management skills, pre-vocational skills)

II. **Curriculum and Instruction**
- Demonstrate knowledge of how to evaluate, select, and develop curriculum materials appropriate for individuals with mild to moderate disabilities, with sensitivity to cultural and linguistic diversity and adaptations and accommodations for individuals with mild to moderate disabilities
- Demonstrate knowledge of how to use local, community, and state resources to assist in developing programs for individuals who are likely to make progress in the general curriculum

- Demonstrate knowledge of how to write appropriate IEP goals and objectives for students with mild to moderate disabilities in academic domains (including vocational) behavioral domains
- Demonstrate knowledge of how to plan instruction based on IEP's, including developing appropriate lesson plans for individuals and groups with mild to moderate disabilities, in academic domains (including vocational) behavioral domains

III. Structuring and Managing the Learning Environment
Learning Environment
- Demonstrate knowledge of behavior management
  - how to implement systematic behavior management plans, using
    - observation
    - recording
    - charting
    - establishment of timelines
    - hierarchies of interventions
    - schedules of reinforcement
    - how to select target behaviors to be changed and identify the critical variables affecting the target behavior

- Demonstrate knowledge of problem-solving and conflict resolution
- Demonstrate knowledge of how to integrate related services into the instructional settings of students with mild to moderate disabilities
- Demonstrate knowledge of how to collaborate with others (including both personnel and families) in planning and providing instruction for students with mild to moderate disabilities

HOW TO TAKE A TEST

You have studied long, hard and conscientiously.

With your official admission card in hand, and your heart pounding, you have been admitted to the examination room.

You note that there are several hundred other applicants in the examination room waiting to take the same test.

They all appear to be equally well prepared.

You know that nothing but your best effort will suffice. The "moment of truth" is at hand: you now have to demonstrate objectively, in writing, your knowledge of content and your understanding of subject matter.

You are fighting the most important battle of your life—to pass and/or score high on an examination which will determine your career and provide the economic basis for your livelihood.

What extra, special things should you know and should you do in taking the examination?

I. YOU MUST PASS AN EXAMINATION

A. WHAT EVERY CANDIDATE SHOULD KNOW
Examination applicants often ask us for help in preparing for the written test. What can I study in advance? What kinds of questions will be asked? How will the test be given? How will the papers be graded?

B. HOW ARE EXAMS DEVELOPED?
Examinations are carefully written by trained technicians who are specialists in the field known as "psychological measurement," in consultation with recognized authorities in the field of work that the test will cover. These experts recommend the subject matter areas or skills to be tested; only those knowledges or skills important to your success on the job are included. The most reliable books and source materials available are used as references. Together, the experts and technicians judge the difficulty level of the questions.
Test technicians know how to phrase questions so that the problem is clearly stated. Their ethics do not permit "trick" or "catch" questions. Questions may have been tried out on sample groups, or subjected to statistical analysis, to determine their usefulness.
Written tests are often used in combination with performance tests, ratings of training and experience, and oral interviews. All of these measures combine to form the best-known means of finding the right person for the right job.

II. HOW TO PASS THE WRITTEN TEST

A. BASIC STEPS

1) Study the announcement

How, then, can you know what subjects to study? Our best answer is: "Learn as much as possible about the class of positions for which you've applied." The exam will test the knowledge, skills and abilities needed to do the work.

Your most valuable source of information about the position you want is the official exam announcement. This announcement lists the training and experience qualifications. Check these standards and apply only if you come reasonably close to meeting them. Many jurisdictions preview the written test in the exam announcement by including a section called "Knowledge and Abilities Required," "Scope of the Examination," or some similar heading. Here you will find out specifically what fields will be tested.

2) Choose appropriate study materials

If the position for which you are applying is technical or advanced, you will read more advanced, specialized material. If you are already familiar with the basic principles of your field, elementary textbooks would waste your time. Concentrate on advanced textbooks and technical periodicals. Think through the concepts and review difficult problems in your field.

These are all general sources. You can get more ideas on your own initiative, following these leads. For example, training manuals and publications of the government agency which employs workers in your field can be useful, particularly for technical and professional positions. A letter or visit to the government department involved may result in more specific study suggestions, and certainly will provide you with a more definite idea of the exact nature of the position you are seeking.

3) Study this book!

III. KINDS OF TESTS

Tests are used for purposes other than measuring knowledge and ability to perform specified duties. For some positions, it is equally important to test ability to make adjustments to new situations or to profit from training. In others, basic mental abilities not dependent on information are essential. Questions which test these things may not appear as pertinent to the duties of the position as those which test for knowledge and information. Yet they are often highly important parts of a fair examination. For very general questions, it is almost impossible to help you direct your study efforts. What we can do is to point out some of the more common of these general abilities needed in public service positions and describe some typical questions.

1) General information

Broad, general information has been found useful for predicting job success in some kinds of work. This is tested in a variety of ways, from vocabulary lists to questions about current events. Basic background in some field of work, such as sociology or economics, may be sampled in a group of questions. Often these are principles which have become familiar to most persons through exposure rather than through formal training. It is difficult to advise you how to study for these questions; being alert to the world around you is our best suggestion.

2) Verbal ability

An example of an ability needed in many positions is verbal or language ability. Verbal ability is, in brief, the ability to use and understand words. Vocabulary and grammar tests are typical measures of this ability. Reading comprehension or paragraph interpretation questions are common in many kinds of civil service tests. You are given a paragraph of written material and asked to find its central meaning.

IV. KINDS OF QUESTIONS

1. Multiple-choice Questions

Most popular of the short-answer questions is the "multiple choice" or "best answer" question. It can be used, for example, to test for factual knowledge, ability to solve problems or judgment in meeting situations found at work.

A multiple-choice question is normally one of three types:
- It can begin with an incomplete statement followed by several possible endings. You are to find the one ending which best completes the statement, although some of the others may not be entirely wrong.
- It can also be a complete statement in the form of a question which is answered by choosing one of the statements listed.
- It can be in the form of a problem – again you select the best answer.

Here is an example of a multiple-choice question with a discussion which should give you some clues as to the method for choosing the right answer:

When an employee has a complaint about his assignment, the action which will best help him overcome his difficulty is to
- A. discuss his difficulty with his coworkers
- B. take the problem to the head of the organization
- C. take the problem to the person who gave him the assignment
- D. say nothing to anyone about his complaint

In answering this question, you should study each of the choices to find which is best. Consider choice "A" – Certainly an employee may discuss his complaint with fellow employees, but no change or improvement can result, and the complaint remains unresolved. Choice "B" is a poor choice since the head of the organization probably does not know what assignment you have been given, and taking your problem to him is known as "going over the head" of the supervisor. The supervisor, or person who made the assignment, is the person who can clarify it or correct any injustice. Choice "C" is, therefore, correct. To say nothing, as in choice "D," is unwise. Supervisors have and interest in knowing the problems employees are facing, and the employee is seeking a solution to his problem.

2. True/False

3. Matching Questions

Matching an answer from a column of choices within another column.

V. RECORDING YOUR ANSWERS

Computer terminals are used more and more today for many different kinds of exams.

For an examination with very few applicants, you may be told to record your answers in the test booklet itself. Separate answer sheets are much more common. If this separate answer sheet is to be scored by machine – and this is often the case – it is highly important that you mark your answers correctly in order to get credit.

VI. BEFORE THE TEST

YOUR PHYSICAL CONDITION IS IMPORTANT

If you are not well, you can't do your best work on tests. If you are half asleep, you can't do your best either. Here are some tips:

1) Get about the same amount of sleep you usually get. Don't stay up all night before the test, either partying or worrying—DON'T DO IT!
2) If you wear glasses, be sure to wear them when you go to take the test. This goes for hearing aids, too.
3) If you have any physical problems that may keep you from doing your best, be sure to tell the person giving the test. If you are sick or in poor health, you relay cannot do your best on any test. You can always come back and take the test some other time.

Common sense will help you find procedures to follow to get ready for an examination. Too many of us, however, overlook these sensible measures. Indeed, nervousness and fatigue have been found to be the most serious reasons why applicants fail to do their best on civil service tests. Here is a list of reminders:

- Begin your preparation early – Don't wait until the last minute to go scurrying around for books and materials or to find out what the position is all about.
- Prepare continuously – An hour a night for a week is better than an all-night cram session. This has been definitely established. What is more, a night a week for a month will return better dividends than crowding your study into a shorter period of time.
- Locate the place of the exam – You have been sent a notice telling you when and where to report for the examination. If the location is in a different town or otherwise unfamiliar to you, it would be well to inquire the best route and learn something about the building.
- Relax the night before the test – Allow your mind to rest. Do not study at all that night. Plan some mild recreation or diversion; then go to bed early and get a good night's sleep.
- Get up early enough to make a leisurely trip to the place for the test – This way unforeseen events, traffic snarls, unfamiliar buildings, etc. will not upset you.
- Dress comfortably – A written test is not a fashion show. You will be known by number and not by name, so wear something comfortable.
- Leave excess paraphernalia at home – Shopping bags and odd bundles will get in your way. You need bring only the items mentioned in the official notice you received; usually everything you need is provided. Do not bring reference books to the exam. They will only confuse those last minutes and be taken away from you when in the test room.

- Arrive somewhat ahead of time – If because of transportation schedules you must get there very early, bring a newspaper or magazine to take your mind off yourself while waiting.
- Locate the examination room – When you have found the proper room, you will be directed to the seat or part of the room where you will sit. Sometimes you are given a sheet of instructions to read while you are waiting. Do not fill out any forms until you are told to do so; just read them and be prepared.
- Relax and prepare to listen to the instructions
- If you have any physical problem that may keep you from doing your best, be sure to tell the test administrator. If you are sick or in poor health, you really cannot do your best on the exam. You can come back and take the test some other time.

VII. AT THE TEST

The day of the test is here and you have the test booklet in your hand. The temptation to get going is very strong. Caution! There is more to success than knowing the right answers. You must know how to identify your papers and understand variations in the type of short-answer question used in this particular examination. Follow these suggestions for maximum results from your efforts:

1) Cooperate with the monitor

The test administrator has a duty to create a situation in which you can be as much at ease as possible. He will give instructions, tell you when to begin, check to see that you are marking your answer sheet correctly, and so on. He is not there to guard you, although he will see that your competitors do not take unfair advantage. He wants to help you do your best.

2) Listen to all instructions

Don't jump the gun! Wait until you understand all directions. In most civil service tests you get more time than you need to answer the questions. So don't be in a hurry. Read each word of instructions until you clearly understand the meaning. Study the examples, listen to all announcements and follow directions. Ask questions if you do not understand what to do.

3) Identify your papers

Civil service exams are usually identified by number only. You will be assigned a number; you must not put your name on your test papers. Be sure to copy your number correctly. Since more than one exam may be given, copy your exact examination title.

4) Plan your time

Unless you are told that a test is a "speed" or "rate of work" test, speed itself is usually not important. Time enough to answer all the questions will be provided, but this does not mean that you have all day. An overall time limit has been set. Divide the total time (in minutes) by the number of questions to determine the approximate time you have for each question.

5) Do not linger over difficult questions

If you come across a difficult question, mark it with a paper clip (useful to have along) and come back to it when you have been through the booklet. One caution if you do this – be sure to skip a number on your answer sheet as well. Check often to be sure that you have not lost your place and that you are marking in the row numbered the same as the question you are answering.

6) Read the questions

Be sure you know what the question asks! Many capable people are unsuccessful because they failed to read the questions correctly.

7) Answer all questions

Unless you have been instructed that a penalty will be deducted for incorrect answers, it is better to guess than to omit a question.

8) Speed tests

It is often better NOT to guess on speed tests. It has been found that on timed tests people are tempted to spend the last few seconds before time is called in marking answers at random – without even reading them – in the hope of picking up a few extra points. To discourage this practice, the instructions may warn you that your score will be "corrected" for guessing. That is, a penalty will be applied. The incorrect answers will be deducted from the correct ones, or some other penalty formula will be used.

9) Review your answers

If you finish before time is called, go back to the questions you guessed or omitted to give them further thought. Review other answers if you have time.

10) Return your test materials

If you are ready to leave before others have finished or time is called, take ALL your materials to the monitor and leave quietly. Never take any test material with you. The monitor can discover whose papers are not complete, and taking a test booklet may be grounds for disqualification.

VIII. EXAMINATION TECHNIQUES

1) Read the general instructions carefully. These are usually printed on the first page of the exam booklet. As a rule, these instructions refer to the timing of the examination; the fact that you should not start work until the signal and must stop work at a signal, etc. If there are any special instructions, such as a choice of questions to be answered, make sure that you note this instruction carefully.

2) When you are ready to start work on the examination, that is as soon as the signal has been given, read the instructions to each question booklet, underline any key words or phrases, such as least, best, outline, describe and the like. In this way you will tend to answer as requested rather than discover on reviewing your paper that you listed without describing, that you selected the worst choice rather than the best choice, etc.

3) If the examination is of the objective or multiple-choice type – that is, each question will also give a series of possible answers: A, B, C or D, and you are called upon to select the best answer and write the letter next to that answer on your answer paper – it is advisable to start answering each question in turn. There may be anywhere from 50 to 100 such questions in the three or four hours allotted and you can see how much time would be taken if you read through all the questions before beginning to answer any. Furthermore, if you

come across a question or group of questions which you know would be difficult to answer, it would undoubtedly affect your handling of all the other questions.

4) If the examination is of the essay type and contains but a few questions, it is a moot point as to whether you should read all the questions before starting to answer any one. Of course, if you are given a choice – say five out of seven and the like – then it is essential to read all the questions so you can eliminate the two that are most difficult. If, however, you are asked to answer all the questions, there may be danger in trying to answer the easiest one first because you may find that you will spend too much time on it. The best technique is to answer the first question, then proceed to the second, etc.

5) Time your answers. Before the exam begins, write down the time it started, then add the time allowed for the examination and write down the time it must be completed, then divide the time available somewhat as follows:
    - If 3-1/2 hours are allowed, that would be 210 minutes. If you have 80 objective-type questions, that would be an average of 2-1/2 minutes per question. Allow yourself no more than 2 minutes per question, or a total of 160 minutes, which will permit about 50 minutes to review.
    - If for the time allotment of 210 minutes there are 7 essay questions to answer, that would average about 30 minutes a question. Give yourself only 25 minutes per question so that you have about 35 minutes to review.

6) The most important instruction is to read each question and make sure you know what is wanted. The second most important instruction is to time yourself properly so that you answer every question. The third most important instruction is to answer every question. Guess if you have to but include something for each question. Remember that you will receive no credit for a blank and will probably receive some credit if you write something in answer to an essay question. If you guess a letter – say "B" for a multiple-choice question – you may have guessed right. If you leave a blank as an answer to a multiple-choice question, the examiners may respect your feelings but it will not add a point to your score. Some exams may penalize you for wrong answers, so in such cases only, you may not want to guess unless you have some basis for your answer.

7) Suggestions
    a. Objective-type questions
       1. Examine the question booklet for proper sequence of pages and questions
       2. Read all instructions carefully
       3. Skip any question which seems too difficult; return to it after all other questions have been answered
       4. Apportion your time properly; do not spend too much time on any single question or group of questions
       5. Note and underline key words – all, most, fewest, least, best, worst, same, opposite, etc.
       6. Pay particular attention to negatives
       7. Note unusual option, e.g., unduly long, short, complex, different or similar in content to the body of the question
       8. Observe the use of "hedging" words – probably, may, most likely, etc.

9. Make sure that your answer is put next to the same number as the question
10. Do not second-guess unless you have good reason to believe the second answer is definitely more correct
11. Cross out original answer if you decide another answer is more accurate; do not erase until you are ready to hand your paper in
12. Answer all questions; guess unless instructed otherwise
13. Leave time for review

b. Essay questions
   1. Read each question carefully
   2. Determine exactly what is wanted. Underline key words or phrases.
   3. Decide on outline or paragraph answer
   4. Include many different points and elements unless asked to develop any one or two points or elements
   5. Show impartiality by giving pros and cons unless directed to select one side only
   6. Make and write down any assumptions you find necessary to answer the questions
   7. Watch your English, grammar, punctuation and choice of words
   8. Time your answers; don't crowd material

8) Answering the essay question

Most essay questions can be answered by framing the specific response around several key words or ideas. Here are a few such key words or ideas:

M's: manpower, materials, methods, money, management
P's: purpose, program, policy, plan, procedure, practice, problems, pitfalls, personnel, public relations
a. Six basic steps in handling problems:
   1. Preliminary plan and background development
   2. Collect information, data and facts
   3. Analyze and interpret information, data and facts
   4. Analyze and develop solutions as well as make recommendations
   5. Prepare report and sell recommendations
   6. Install recommendations and follow up effectiveness

   b. Pitfalls to avoid
   1. Taking things for granted – A statement of the situation does not necessarily imply that each of the elements is necessarily true; for example, a complaint may be invalid and biased so that all that can be taken for granted is that a complaint has been registered
   2. Considering only one side of a situation – Wherever possible, indicate several alternatives and then point out the reasons you selected the best one
   3. Failing to indicate follow up – Whenever your answer indicates action on your part, make certain that you will take proper follow-up action to see how successful your recommendations, procedures or actions turn out to be
   4. Taking too long in answering any single question – Remember to time your answers properly

EXAMINATION SECTION

EXAMINATION SECTION
TEST 1

DIRECTIONS: Each question or incomplete statement is followed by several suggested answers or completions. Select the one that BEST answers the question or completes the statement. *PRINT THE LETTER OF THE CORRECT ANSWER IN THE SPACE AT THE RIGHT.*

1. Which of the following is most essential to implementing P.L. 94-142? 1._____

    A. A continuum of services for handicapped children
    B. Full funding by federal government
    C. Full funding by state government
    D. Mainstreaming of handicapped children

2. According to Public Law 94-142, (The Education for All Handicapped Children Act of 1975), handicapped children must be evaluated 2._____

    A. at least once a year
    B. as requested by school or parents
    C. every three years, or more often, if warranted or requested
    D. when the handicapped child moves from one grade to the next

3. The BEST activity for teaching social competencies to handicapped children is 3._____

    A. visits to regular classrooms
    B. interaction with normal peers
    C. learning to accept handicapped classmates
    D. sharing school playground experiences with normal peers

4. Each child in the classroom is asked to choose two classmates with whom he/she would like to play. This technique is used in 4._____

    A. sociometric analysis   B. behavior analysis
    C. contingency management   D. independence surveys

5. Aphasia is characterized by 5._____

    A. awkwardness of fine and gross motor movements, especially those involved with balance and posture
    B. loss or impairment of the ability to understand or formulate language
    C. abnormally low blood sugar levels and frequent feelings of weakness and fatigue
    D. a congenital midline defect resulting from a bifurcation of the bony spinal column

6. The Rosenthal and Jacobsen study, reported in their book "Pygmalion in the Classroom," experimentally demonstrated what the authors call the "self-fulfilling prophecy." Attempts by others to replicate this study generally have shown that the conclusions reached by Rosenthal and Jacobsen have 6._____

    A. not been verified for all children
    B. been verified for all children
    C. been applicable only to handicapped children
    D. been applicable only to non-handicapped children

7. Perseveration refers to a child's inability to

   A. discontinue a response pattern once it is started
   B. repeat complex sentences
   C. focus visually on a fixed point
   D. consistently complete assigned tasks

8. A child who exhibits behaviors of distractibility, hyper-activity and perseveration is manifesting signs most characteristic of _____ syndrome.

   A. Turner's   B. Down   C. Jacob's   D. Strauss

9. When a child has a grand mal seizure in the classroom, the FIRST thing a teacher should do is

   A. send the class out of the room
   B. have the office call an ambulance
   C. force a pencil between his teeth and open the shirt at the neck
   D. move away nearby desks and other furniture

10. The automatic involuntary repetition of heard phrases, words and sentences is known as

    A. jargon   B. echolalia   C. lalling   D. transference

11. Children have *probably* attained normal gross motor adequacy if they can jump, hop on one foot, walk a curb or low wall and catch or throw a ball by age

    A. 3   B. 7   C. 9   D. 5

12. A child who suffers from ataxia is *most likely* to manifest

    A. disturbance in balance which is reflected in posture and gait
    B. difficulty in purposeful movement which causes poor motor skills
    C. slow involuntary movement of a paralyzed limb which results in tremors
    D. simultaneous contraction of the flexor and extensor muscles which causes rigidity

13. The handicap *most commonly* associated with rubella is

    A. hearing loss   B. neurological impairment
    C. cardiac defect   D. visual dysfunction

14. If records from the Committee on the Handicapped state that a newly admitted pupil is suffering from scoliosis, you should plan for a pupil who has

    A. brittleness of the skeletal system
    B. slipped epiphysis
    C. cancer of the spinal column
    D. lateral curvature of the spine

15. A record refers to a pupil as "emotionally labile." The teacher should be prepared to work with a pupil who

    A. is generally shy and withdrawn
    B. is generally cheerful even in inappropriate circumstances
    C. suffers excessively from sibling rivalry and projects jealousy to peer surrogates
    D. has frequent and unanticipated swings in mood

16. The symptom *most likely* to be manifested by a pupil with dysarthria is

    A. poor speech production and articulation
    B. an inability to remember words, sequences or syntactical structures
    C. motor difficulties affecting gait and use of hands
    D. inability to form concepts

17. Hyperkinetic is a term that describes a pupil who exhibits

    A. abnormal tightness of muscles not at work
    B. symptoms of hyperopia
    C. symptoms of myopia
    D. excessive motor activity, inattention and impulsivity

18. A test that measures a child's perceptual motor abilities is the

    A. Peabody Individual Achievement Test
    B. Thematic Apperception Test
    C. Bender Gestalt Test
    D. Detroit Test of Learning Aptitude

19. A teacher who needs to know more about a child's ability to extract relevant sensory data from the environment and relay it in a consistent and integrated fashion to the higher levels of the central nervous system should study material concerning

    A. coordination   B. sensation
    C. maturation   D. perception

20. Norm-referenced devices have an advantage over criterion-referenced devices when the *primary* purpose of testing is to determine

    A. mastery level of individual skills
    B. instructional objectives
    C. mastery level in relation to peers
    D. daily behavior inventory

21. For which age group are intelligence tests LEAST valid and reliable?

    A. Pre-school grades   B. K-6 grades
    C. 7th-9th grades   D. 10th-12th grades

22. An evaluative teaching system that summarizes changes in performance over time through direct and daily measurement of performance rate is known as

    A. precision teaching   B. management by objectives
    C. clinical teaching   D. multi-modality teaching

23. The standard deviation is a measure of

    A. reliability   B. consistency
    C. variability   D. regression

24. What is the median of the following set of test scores: 64-50-40-34-22-18-13?

    A. 33.0 B. 34.0 C. 38.5 D. 40.0

25. The teacher's FIRST step in developing a mathematics diagnostic inventory is to

    A. determine time and place for testing
    B. choose the content to be assesssed
    C. compare sequence and format with a standardized test
    D. review the mathematics series used by the school

26. The classroom use of projective techniques is best illustrated by

    A. audio-visual aids   B. interest inventories
    C. patterning   D. puppetry

27. Which of the following terms is MOST closely related to the use of behavior modification techniques?

    A. Insight development   B. Gestalt
    C. Cognitive   D. Operant conditioning

28. As a behavior management technique, time-out for inappropriate behavior is MOST effective when used

    A. in concert with other aversive reinforcers for inappropriate behavior
    B. in isolation from other procedures
    C. in concert with reinforcement for appropriate behavior
    D. for periods of time determined by the pupils

29. Which of the following statements made by a teacher would produce the LEAST confusion in student behavior?

    A. "George, stop kicking the chair."
    B. "George, I must tell you again to stop that."
    C. "George, what should you be doing now?"
    D. "George, you should be doing what the rest of the class is doing now."

30. The teacher who emphasizes effective techniques in the classroom is *primarily* concerned with pupils'

    A. feelings and emotions   B. observable behavior
    C. gross motor development   D. genetic development

KEY (CORRECT ANSWERS)

1. A
2. C
3. B
4. A
5. B

6. B
7. A
8. D
9. D
10. B

11. D
12. D
13. C
14. D
15. D

16. A
17. D
18. C
19. D
20. C

21. A
22. B
23. C
24. B
25. B

26. D
27. D
28. C
29. C
30. B

TEST 2

DIRECTIONS: Each question or incomplete statement is followed by several suggested answers or completions. Select the one that BEST answers the question or completes the statement. *PRINT THE LETTER OF THE CORRECT ANSWER IN THE SPACE AT THE RIGHT.*

1. Carl Bereiter and Siegfried Engelmann, who developed the DISTAR program for teaching "culturally disadvantaged" children, based their work on the premise that these children own language effectively *only* in

    A. obtaining and transmitting information
    B. meeting social and material needs
    C. monitoring their own behavior
    D. verbal reasoning

    1.___

2. The BEST example of a well-stated specific educational objective is:

    A. Have each pupil in the occupational skills class improve self-concept through individually planned success experiences using standards that are part of the "mainstream" program.
    B. Have each pupil in the occupational skills class increase reading comprehension through individually planned vocabulary study and word recognition drill for a minimum of 15 minutes each day.
    C. Provide each pupil in the occupational skills class with the functional reading skills and vocabulary necessary for employment in low skill occupational areas.
    D. Have each pupil in the occupational skills class construct an acrylic picture frame according to a distributed plan, making fewer than four correctable errors and with all measurements within 1/8 inch tolerance.

    2.___

3. Current practice in programming career education for handicapped children is based on the premise that career education should begin

    A. in the primary grades
    B. in the junior high school
    C. after children have developed proficiency in reading and mathematics
    D. in the 10th year of school

    3.___

4. The behavior modification technique of desensitization is MOST effective with a child who is

    A. perseverative   B. fearful   C. distractible   D. aggressive

    4.___

5. Assume you are teaching a unit on the development of democratic institutions. A short range goal is understanding the principle that the head of a nation, like everyone else, is bound by law. The document that you should use in pre-planning this unit is the

    A. Magna Carta (The Great Charter of England)
    B. Constitution (United States)
    C. Declaration of Independence (United States)
    D. Declaration of Rights of Man (France)

    5.___

6. A teacher is planning a unit on economic systems. When planning a section of the unit on the system of free enterprise based on limited role of government in the economy, the teacher should cite as a proponent of this type of system the writings of

   A. John Kenneth Galbraith
   B. Friedrich Engels
   C. John Maynard Keynes
   D. Adam Smith

7. A teacher is planning a unit on civil rights and their relevance to the daily lives of the pupils. When planning, the teacher consults the book "UP From Slavery" by

   A. Frederick Douglass
   B. Booker T. Washington
   C. Nat Turner
   D. John Brown

8. A teacher plans a lesson in the use of primary source material to investigate the background of the Louisiana Purchase. Which of the following would be MOST helpful as a *primary* source of information?

   A. The text of the Dred Scott Decision
   B. Goode's World Atlas
   C. Collier's Encyclopedia
   D. The Journals of Lewis and Clark

9. A teacher plans a unit in social studies, emphasizing the link between individuals and the development of historical ideas. Which one of the following *correctly* pairs a proponent of an ideology with a historical trend?

   A. Mohandas Gandhi - Militarism
   B. Count von Metternich - Revolution
   C. Benjamin Disraeli - Colonialism
   D. Samual Adams - Pacifism

10. In a unit on How We Learn About The Past, a teacher who uses simulated artifacts and material remains is following a method that *most closely* approximates the method used by

    A. archeologists
    B. historians
    C. enzymologists
    D. zoologists

11. In order to achieve mathematic objectives in division, pupils should be taught the BASIC principle of division as

    A. repeated multiplication
    B. the inverse of addition
    C. repeated subtraction
    D. the inverse of subtraction

12. A teacher is planning a lesson on scale drawing and has the pupils measure the floor of their classroom. If the room measures 28 feet x 36 feet and 1/4 inch = 1 foot, the dimensions of the scale should be

    A. 7 feet by 9 feet
    B. 112 inches by 144 inches
    C. 112 feet by 144 feet
    D. 7 inches by 9 inches

13. The approach that emphasizes the learning of conceptual knowledge of the basic structure of mathematics through observation and discovery of mathematical relationships is

    A. Milton Bradley Flash Cards
    B. SRA's Criterion - Referenced Measurement Program
    C. Distar Arithmetic
    D. Cuisenaire - Gattegno Rods

14. The celebration of Bastille Day in Prance has its equivalent in our _____ Day.

    A. Independence   B. Memorial
    C. Labor   D. Veterans

15. In planning a lesson on the rotation of the earth on its axis, the teacher should lead the class to calculate that the earth must pass through how many degress of longitude in in one hour?

    A. 15   B. 24   C. 180   D. 360

16. In teaching a lesson on the consequence of the earth's rotation on its axis, the teacher should lead the pupils to infer that this rotation causes

    A. changes in season   B. night and day
    C. the phases of the moon   D. tidal changes

17. In planning a unit on how green plants produce nutrients necessary for human life, the teacher should be aware that this process is called

    A. photosynthesis   B. absorption
    C. osmosis   D. oxidation

18. When teaching the use of contextual clues in word recognition, the teacher should explain that word(s)

    A. recognition may be obtained from the sense or meaning of the rest of the sentence or paragraph
    B. may be recognized by their shape or form
    C. may have similar combinations of letters and sounds
    D. may have more than one meaning

19. The MOST essential requirement of an individualized reading program is

    A. the availability of a wide range of reading materials
    B. self-evaluation
    C. the use of programmed materials
    D. symbol-sound correspondence

20. A teacher is planning a unit on figures of speech as part of a communication arts program. Which of the following is an INCORRECT definition of a figure of speech?

    A. Irony expresses a meaning opposite to the usual meaning.
    B. A metaphor is a comparison of one thing with something different, using the words as or like.
    C. Hyperbole is a fancifully exaggerated statement.
    D. Alliteration is the repetition of initial sounds.

21. In planning to teach children how to tell time, the objective that should be taught last in sequence is to

    A. determine the functions of the large and small hands of a clock
    B. tell time by five minute intervals
    C. distinguish the "past" and "before" sides of a clock
    D. identify half-past the hour

22. In teaching a lesson on time zones, the instructional goal of the teacher should be that the pupils conclude that time zones are determined by

    A. degress of longitude
    B. degrees of latitude
    C. inclination of the earth
    D. seasonal fluctuations in the amount of daylight

23. In a science lesson, the teacher should demonstrate the SMALLEST part of a compound that still retains the properties of the compound is a(n)

    A. element   B. atom
    C. molecule   D. quark

24. A teacher plans to demonstrate in a science unit that an object in motion tends to maintain its motion. The teacher would be demonstrating the principle of

    A. inertia   B. gravitation
    C. attraction   D. magnetic induction

25. A teacher is planning a unit that will alert the class to the fact that some maps have inaccuracies. In pre-planning, the teacher studying a map using the Mercator projection should see that the areas MOST exaggerated in size are near the

    A. north and south poles   B. equator
    C. temperate zones   D. international date line

26. A teacher is developing a unit on religious intolerance which sometimes exists among those who have sought religious tolerance for themselves. In planning this unit, the teacher should read material describing the banishment of Roger Williams and Anna Hutchinson from the colony of

    A. Rhode Island   B. Pennsylvania
    C. Connecticut   D. Massachusetts

27. Which of the following sentences should a class identify as containing a grammatical error?

    A. I am sure she told you and me to meet her at the theater.
    B. If a child and either one of her parents don't attend, please schedule another date.
    C. I believe that neither one of us knows the answer.
    D. Everyone of the actors must memorize their script.

28. A teacher is planning to develop condensed and/or simplified versions of short stories with surprise endings for her class of handicapped children. Which one of the following authors is the best source of material for this purpose? 28._____

   A. O. Henry
   B. Conan Boyle
   C. George Eliot
   D. James Thurber

29. Which one of the following is a CORRECT statement of a short-term objective in teaching the approximate weight equivalent of a pound and a kilogram? One 29._____

   A. pound is a little more than twice as heavy as one kilogram.
   B. kilogram is a little more than twice as heavy as one pound.
   C. kilogram is about 50% heavier than one pound.
   D. pound is about 50% heavier than one kilogram.

30. A teacher is planning a lesson on conversion from metric to English units of measure. The class should be led to calculate that 36 liters of gasoline are approximately _____ gallons. 30._____

   A. 5   B. 10   C. 15   D. 20

KEY (CORRECT ANSWERS)

1.	B	16.	B
2.	D	17.	A
3.	A	18.	A
4.	B	19.	B
5.	A	20.	B
6.	D	21.	B
7.	A	22.	A
8.	D	23.	C
9.	C	24.	A
10.	A	25.	A
11.	A	26.	A
12.	D	27.	B
13.	D	28.	A
14.	A	29.	C
15.	A	30.	C

EXAMINATION SECTION
TEST 1

DIRECTIONS: Each question or incomplete statement is followed by several suggested answers or completions. Select the one that BEST answers the question or completes the statement. *PRINT THE LETTER OF THE CORRECT ANSWER IN THE SPACE AT THE RIGHT.*

1. The key concept in guidance for the physically handicapped is 1.____

   A. occupational placement
   B. subject matter mastery
   C. realistic evaluation
   D. avocational development

2. Studies of the school achievement of physically handicapped pupils tend to indicate that 2.____

   A. there is no difference between the achievement of normal children and that of physically handicapped children
   B. physically handicapped children do not achieve as well as non-handicapped children
   C. physically handicapped children achieve slightly above the level of normal children of the same intellectual level
   D. comparisons of physically handicapped and normal children cannot be undertaken because equated groups cannot be formed

3. Of the following, the MOST important elements determining the difficulty of reading material are 3.____

   A. average sentence length and number of difficult words
   B. paragraph size and number of sentences
   C. number of new words and length of new words
   D. length of story and sentence complexity

4. In working with Joseph, a nine-year-old physically handicapped boy, his teacher finds that he does not know the meaning of numbers.
The teacher should 4.____

   A. have him use a good workbook
   B. provide him with thinking cards
   C. return to the manipulation of representative materials
   D. ask his parents to help him with drills on number facts

5. Which one of the following pairs of examples illustrates the concept of *exchanging* in developmental mathematics? 5.____

   A. $\begin{array}{cc} 6 & 7 \\ \times 7 & \times 6 \end{array}$
   B. $\begin{array}{cc} 16 & 16 \\ +27 & +26 \end{array}$
   C. $4\overline{)12}\quad 12 \div 4$
   D. $\begin{array}{cc} 27 & 27 \\ -14 & -17 \end{array}$

6. Tommy shows considerable difficulty in working out new words in reading. Miss Jones can BEST discover the cause of this weakness by 6.____

A. listening to Tommy's oral reading and carefully noting his errors
B. administering a formal oral reading test, such as Gray's Oral Paragraphs
C. giving Tommy a diagnostic test in phonics
D. determining Tommy's sight vocabulary through a series of informal tests

7. Of the following, which disease requires STRICTEST control of the time interval between meals?

    A. Rheumatic fever   B. Allergy
    C. Diabetes   D. Epilepsy

8. A handicapped pupil who has lost the movement of his fingers but who still retains good movement of his wrist and arm should

    A. be given exercises by the teacher to restore the lost movement
    B. be excused from written work because it would be too frustrating
    C. be taught to write using a pencil attached to the hand
    D. not be expected to learn as well as other children

9. In teaching speech to a child who is an athetoid, the teacher should stress the importance of

    A. clear enunciation
    B. tongue placement
    C. keeping the head steady
    D. swallowing and speaking on expiration

10. Paul, an eight-year-old child with a diagnosis of organic brain damage, has not learned to read despite the fact that he is eager to do so.
    The teacher should

    A. have him build a picture dictionary
    B. give him concrete geometric forms to manipulate
    C. give him work in phonic analysis
    D. start work on building a sight vocabulary with him

11. Alice, a quadriplegic, has difficulty in turning the pages of her textbook.
    The teacher should

    A. turn the pages for her
    B. limit the use of the textbook and stress oral work
    C. demonstrate the proper way in which to turn pages
    D. use clips to weight pages to be turned

12. Of the following, which item is MOST apt to be associated with cerebral palsy?

    A. Lounge chair   B. Hockey stick
    C. Flannel board   D. Football helmet

13. A child with cerebral palsy frequently learns to write by using special equipment. This equipment should include a

    A. tachistoscope
    B. tens frame

C. flannel board
D. typewriter with a covered keyboard

14. David, a twelve-year-old boy with muscular dystrophy, has trouble getting his wheelchair close to the table in order to write.
    The teacher should suggest that he use a

    A. board on the arms of his wheelchair as a desk top
    B. regular chair when he is at the table
    C. semicircular table that is made for this purpose
    D. clipboard

15. Which one of the following would be MOST useful for a child who is a diplegic?

    A. Electric page turner   B. Mirror
    C. Counting box   D. Squared material

16. Children with braces and in wheelchairs find it difficult to paint at easels because they must remain seated. The equipment which would provide a solution for this problem is

    A. a standing box
    B. an Everest and Jennings wheelchair
    C. parallel bars at the correct height for the easel
    D. an easel with adjustable heights

17. Many physically handicapped children who were limited to home instruction fifteen years ago now attend school because provision has been made for

    A. motorized wheelchairs
    B. movable furniture in classrooms
    C. buses with hydraulic lifts
    D. special automobile service

18. Of the following, which disease is MUCH MORE prevalent now than it was twenty years ago?

    A. Poliomyelitis   B. Spina bifida
    C. Hemophilia   D. Infectious hepatitis

19. Auto-education or self-teaching, the forerunner of *programmed instruction,* was the keynote of a system devised by

    A. Binet   B. Itard   C. Seguin   D. Montessori

20. In recent years, the MOST important single factor in the establishment and expansion of educational services for the physically handicapped has been

    A. research work in the colleges and universities
    B. increased interest on the part of state and federal agencies
    C. pressure from parent organizations
    D. contributions of professional organizations

21. Which one of the following approaches to the treatment of epilepsy has been MOST successful in recent years?

    A. Drug therapy
    B. Special diets
    C. Psychotherapy
    D. Shock therapy

22. Early research in the education of brain-injured children without motor handicaps was done by

    A. Cruickshank   B. Barker   C. Lehtinen   D. Fouracre

23. Books describing methods and techniques in teaching the neurologically impaired have been published by

    A. Kirk and Lehtinen
    B. Cruickshank and Strauss
    C. Gallagher and Kephart
    D. Strauss and Johnson

24. The treatment of cardiac children has changed in the last twenty years. Authorities now recommend

    A. lengthened periods of bed rest and quick resumption of normal activities
    B. lengthened periods of bed rest and gradual resumption of normal activities
    C. shortened periods of bed rest and quick resumption of normal activities
    D. shortened periods of bed rest and gradual resumption of normal activities

25. In recent years, particular attention has been paid to the educational problem presented by

    A. the brain injured
    B. hemophiliacs
    C. the orthopedically handicapped
    D. children with muscular dystrophy

26. Which one of the following procedures has given rise to the GREATEST amount of controversy among experts in the field of special education?

    A. Developing special programs of education for home-bound pupils
    B. Providing special facilities for preschool physically handicapped children
    C. Placing handicapped children in regular rather than in special classes
    D. Placing emotionally disturbed children on home instruction

27. The exact cause of rheumatic fever is unknown, but in susceptible individuals, an attack is frequently preceded by

    A. a respiratory streptococcal infection
    B. recurrent migraine disturbance
    C. a violent spasm of intestinal distress
    D. sustained and intense feverish disorder

28. Which one of the following may result in brain damage and mental deficiency?

    A. Meningitis and encephalitis
    B. Poliomyelitis and chorea
    C. Scarlet fever and enuresis
    D. Rheumatic fever and arthritis

29. The MOST frequent glandular condition associated with mental retardation is a deficiency in the functioning of the _____ gland.

    A. pineal   B. thyroid   C. pituitary   D. adrenal

30. Some authorities maintain that the inability of the body to utilize a vitamin properly is a causative factor in

    A. epilepsy   B. muscular dystrophy
    C. chorea   D. achondroplasia

31. Glandular fever is sometimes referred to as

    A. mononucleosis   B. myasthenia gravis
    C. monoplegia   D. ileitis

32. A metabolic disease in which there is persistent hyperglycemia, excessive thirst, and loss of weight is

    A. cancer   B. heart disease
    C. diabetes   D. Addison's disease

33. Insulin, which enables the body to utilize and store sugar properly, is produced by the

    A. liver   B. islands of Langerhans
    C. spleen   D. bone marrow

34. Victims of rheumatic fever are prone to develop chronic forms of

    A. dyspepsia and dysphagia
    B. sore throats and tonsilitis
    C. migraine and asthma
    D. intestinal and muscular disorder

35. A child with a positive EEG reading is likely to have

    A. asthma   B. rheumatic fever
    C. convulsive disorders   D. nephritis

36. Spasticity may reduce a child's ability to respond accurately to a teacher's questions requiring

    A. use of the sense of touch
    B. recall of prior learning
    C. knowledge of subject matter
    D. familiarity with domestic routines

37. Of the following, which child is MOST apt to encounter difficulty in handling spatial relationships?
The child with

    A. spina bifida   B. ulcerative colitis
    C. Pott's disease   D. cerebral palsy

38. Which one of the following is characterized by involuntary, abnormal movements in the extremities?

    A. Myositus
    B. Rheumatic fever
    C. Athetosis
    D. Scoliosis

39. Of the following, the disease that is believed to have strong psychosomatic implications is

    A. colitis   B. diabetes   C. anemia   D. hepatitis

40. Which one of the following is a congenital disease that involves the internal organs of the body?

    A. Cystic fibrosis
    B. Nephritis
    C. Tuberculosis
    D. Synovitis

KEY (CORRECT ANSWERS)

1. C	11. D	21. A	31. A
2. B	12. D	22. C	32. C
3. A	13. D	23. C	33. B
4. C	14. A	24. D	34. B
5. B	15. A	25. A	35. C
6. C	16. D	26. C	36. A
7. C	17. C	27. A	37. D
8. C	18. D	28. A	38. C
9. D	19. D	29. B	39. A
10. B	20. C	30. B	40. A

TEST 2

DIRECTIONS: Each question or incomplete statement is followed by several suggested answers or completions. Select the one that BEST answers the question or completes the statement. *PRINT THE LETTER OF THE CORRECT ANSWER IN THE SPACE AT THE RIGHT.*

1. A device that was developed for intercommunication between a homebound child and the classroom is the

    A. Linguaphone
    B. Executone
    C. CC (Closed Circuit) Intercom
    D. Recordax

    1._____

2. Of the following, the BEST way a teacher of physically handicapped children can find out about their previous progress is by

    A. examining test results
    B. examining units undertaken in previous grades
    C. studying their cumulative record cards
    D. speaking to their parents

    2._____

3. Test norms provide a basis for ascertaining where a pupil

    A. should rank in relation to a group
    B. can rank were he to develop good study habits
    C. ranks in relation to a group
    D. will rank under normal instruction

    3._____

4. With each succeeding year, until maximum development is attained, the amount of increment in mental growth is

    A. less than in the preceding year
    B. more than in the preceding year
    C. at about the same rate throughout life
    D. quite variable so that no predictions can be made

    4._____

5. An index of a pupil's learning efficiency can be determined through examining the relationship of

    A. chronological age to achievement
    B. achievement to interest
    C. mental age to achievement
    D. achievement to grade placement

    5._____

6. The following are three examples of anecdotal records which have been written by teachers:

    I. *John is continually taking things that belong to other boys in the class. He is the biggest sneak-thief I have ever taught.*
    II. *This morning John started a fight with Elaine when my back was turned. you have to watch him every minute or he gets into trouble.*
    III. *When called on this morning, John gave an excellent answer to a difficult question. He has yet to volunteer any information in class.*

    6._____

If the above behavior descriptions were arranged in order of their adequacy, from best to poorest, the CORRECT sequence would be

    A. III, II, I
    B. III, I, II
    C. II, III, I
    D. II, I, III

7. Of the following, the MOST effective contribution a teacher can make in meeting the problems of a handicapped child is to

    A. develop in the child awareness of his limitations
    B. set realistic goals for the child
    C. cooperate with the social agency that is taking major responsibility for planning with the family
    D. shield the child from emotional shock

8. Jimmy starts to repeat the speech of his mother (echolalia) and to mimic his father's physical activities (echopraxia). Both echolalia and exchopraxia may be viewed as infantile forms of

    A. projection
    B. identification
    C. reaction formation
    D. rationalization

9. The teacher of the physically handicapped who has a sound mental health point of view will

    A. accept the fact that physical handicap is a limitation that cannot be overcome
    B. be more solicitous of the child with a handicap than of other children
    C. look upon the physical limitation as one of the many aspects of the child's developmental history
    D. realize that the handicap is a disabling factor that calls for compensatory treatment by the teacher

10. Which one of the following children is usually given the LEAST attention by the teacher of the physically handicapped? The child who

    A. is always daydreaming
    B. is always clowning
    C. never completes an assignment
    D. continually sucks his thumb

11. Of the following, which mechanism of adjustment is FREQUENTLY noted among handicapped pupils?

    A. Exhibitionism
    B. Animism
    C. Introversion
    D. Conversion hysteria

12. Mary, a fourteen-year-old physically handicapped pupil who is overweight and unattractive, recently began to use an excessive amount of make-up. Her lips are drawn in an exaggerated manner, and her eyebrows are plucked and penciled.
Her behavior should be looked upon as a form of

    A. regression
    B. compensation
    C. introjection
    D. identification

13. Studies of use of rewards and punishments in learning a skill have indicated that learning is likely to be achieved MOST rapidly when

A. the learner is punished for an occasional wrong response
B. the learner is punished when he consistently gives wrong responses
C. the learner is rewarded for correct responses
D. no systematic use is made of rewards and punishments

14. Studies of the course of forgetting indicate that the GREATEST amount of learned material is forgotten

    A. after a period of disuse
    B. after the first attempt at recall
    C. after the first attempt at recognition
    D. immediately after the material has been learned

15. Relearning is generally MOST efficient when

    A. the original material is relearned as a whole
    B. discrete parts of the material are relearned in sections
    C. the original material is organized in a different sequence and then relearned as a whole
    D. the original material is organized in a different sequence and then relearned in sections

16. Of the following, the man who stressed the principle that the chief prerequisite to learning is the readiness of the individual to learn was

    A. Kohler   B. Ebbinghaus   C. Watson   D. Thorndike

17. Of the following, the MOST effective form of motivation for school work is

    A. intrinsic interest in the subject matter being studied
    B. praise by the teacher
    C. recognition in the form of a school honor roll and the like
    D. fear of failure

18. A useful method of teaching spelling, developed by Grace M. Fernald, is known as the _____ method.

    A. test-study-test   B. audiophonic
    C. kinesthetic   D. visual-motor

19. Written lessons in spelling are more effective than oral lessons in establishing recall because the written approach

    A. is more meaningful than the oral
    B. lends itself to greater variety of presentation
    C. presents words in the form in which they will be used
    D. appeals to many senses at once

20. Which of the following approaches should be MINIMIZED in teaching physically handicapped pupils how to prepare a good research report?

    A. Using the table of contents and the index to find the right passages
    B. Making verbatim transcriptions of facts
    C. Skimming for the facts desired
    D. Conveying information effectively in a variety of forms

21. To give her pupils a basic sight vocabulary, the teacher of a physically handicapped child should be guided by a word list compiled by

   A. Horn   B. Cunningham   C. Dolch   D. Seashore

21._____

22. Johnny, a twelve-year-old physically handicapped child, uses manuscript writing legibly and neatly. Attempts to make the transition to cursive writing have shown fair results but Johnny is antagonistic and prefers to continue with his manuscript writing.
His teacher should

   A. withdraw some privilege until he switches to cursive writing
   B. continue with cursive writing and offer appropriate rewards
   C. explain the need for cursive writing in the business world and continue it
   D. permit him to use manuscript writing

22._____

23. The PRIMARY aim in developing a functional spelling program with the physically handicapped pupil is to help him

   A. read words most frequently used in his writing
   B. learn words which he will encounter in his reading
   C. acquire an efficient method of studying new words
   D. spell correctly the words he will use in his writing

23._____

24. An athetoid cerebral palsied child has a tendency to mirror writing.
The teacher should

   A. recommend that the child have an eye examination
   B. provide a mirror so that the material can be read
   C. check for left-handedness
   D. ask for an evaluation by the Bureau of Child Guidance

24._____

25. Of the following, the BEST exercise to overcome shallow breathing in a cerebral palsied child is

   A. dramatizing the THREE LITTLE PIGS
   B. imitating a rag doll
   C. singing A DILLAR, A DOLLAR
   D. reciting DING, DONG, DELL

25._____

26. In providing learning activities for the child showing a spastic type of cerebral palsy, the MOST important factor in achieving satisfactory pupil progress is

   A. variety
   B. figure-background integration
   C. dissociation of stimulus and response
   D. repetition

26._____

27. Brain-injured children tend to function MOST successfully in rooms that are

   A. bustling with activity
   B. free from stimulation
   C. decorated with bright colors
   D. characterized by a permissive climate

27._____

28. Which one of the following types of handicapped children would be MOST likely to require a page turner?
    The child who is a

    A. unilateral amputee
    B. post-polio case with residual weakness in the hamstrings and gastrocnemius
    C. spastic quadriplegic
    D. left hemiplegic

29. In maintaining information concerning health problems of pupils, which one of the following conditions is recorded ONLY in a confidential file?

    A. Amputation   B. Tuberculosis
    C. Diabetes   D. Ringworm

30. A child suffering from convulsive seizures develops a deviate behavior pattern.
    The teacher should

    A. maintain a *log* of the child's deviate behavior
    B. enter a note of unusual incidents on the Pupil Health Card
    C. itemize incidents on the Cumulative Record Card
    D. send a note to the principal each time the child is disruptive

31. A teacher may anticipate involuntary motions of hands, arms, and legs from a pupil with a diagnosis of

    A. muscular dystrophy   B. brachial birth palsy
    C. athetosis   D. epiphysis

32. Studies of the relationship between emotional disturbance and intellectual development or functioning have established that emotional disturbance USUALLY

    A. has little significant effect on the quality of mental functioning
    B. has a significant effect on the level of mental functioning
    C. affects the quality but not the level of mental functioning
    D. affects the level but not the quality of mental functioning

33. Arteriosclerosis is a disturbance of the _____ system.

    A. skeletal   B. endocrine   C. nervous   D. circulatory

34. Of the following disorders, which one is NOT a form of cerebral palsy?

    A. Little's disease   B. Athetosis
    C. Mitral stenosis   D. Spastic paralysis

35. The chin is rotated away from the side of the short, prominent muscle; the head is tilted toward the affected side.
    These symptoms are characteristic of

    A. talipes   B. torticollis   C. ligamentitis   D. bursitis

36. A patient designated by a physician as *Class IID* is suffering from

    A. diabetes   B. polio
    C. tuberculosis   D. heart disease

37. A dorsal curvature is GENERALLY referred to as 37.____

   A. lordosis B. kyphosis C. scoliosis D. curatosis

38. A disease that USUALLY occurs in overweight boys and girls between the ages of ten and thirteen years and is characterized by upper tibial epiphysitis is known as _____ disease. 38.____

   A. Pott's
   B. Charcot-Tooth's
   C. Little's
   D. Osgood-Schlatter's

39. A child whose walk is characterized by a scissors gait, with inward rotation and adduction of the legs, is PROBABLY suffering from 39.____

   A. Erb's palsy
   B. spasticity
   C. osteogenesis imperfecta
   D. spina bifida

40. Which of the following children will GENERALLY be placed in a regular class rather than in a health conservation class? 40.____

   A. Cardiopathic children
   B. Epileptic children
   C. Children with orthopedic handicaps
   D. Tuberculosis children

KEY (CORRECT ANSWERS)

1. B	11. C	21. C	31. C
2. C	12. B	22. D	32. B
3. C	13. C	23. D	33. D
4. A	14. D	24. C	34. C
5. C	15. A	25. A	35. B
6. A	16. D	26. D	36. D
7. C	17. A	27. B	37. B
8. B	18. C	28. C	38. D
9. C	19. C	29. B	39. B
10. A	20. B	30. A	40. B

TEST 3

DIRECTIONS: Each question or incomplete statement is followed by several suggested answers or completions. Select the one that BEST answers the question or completes the statement. *PRINT THE LETTER OF THE CORRECT ANSWER IN THE SPACE AT THE RIGHT.*

1. In seeking to determine whether a physically handicapped junior high school pupil is ready for the next developmental level in mathematics, which of the following procedures will the teacher find of LEAST value?

    A. Listening to his explanation as to how he arrived at an estimate
    B. Keeping a record of his homework performance
    C. Observing him as he works on practice materials
    D. Examining his test results

2. Of the following, the MOST important factor in the physically handicapped child's successful transition from manuscript to cursive writing is his ability to

    A. hold his pen or pencil correctly
    B. read on a third grade level
    C. read words in cursive writing
    D. write words rather than isolated letters

3. The sequence of experiences for teaching a basic number fact to physically handicapped pupils includes these stages:
    I. Objectify the fact with markers or other manipulative materials
    II. Write the fact in symbolic form
    III. Show the fact by use of real objects or pictures
    IV. Reproduce the fact by drawings of dots or x's
    What is the CORRECT sequence of the above stages?

    A. II, III, IV, I   B. III, I, IV, II
    C. I, IV, III, II   D. III, IV, I, II

4. Growth in ability to read independently with understanding and appreciation develops MOST consistently when the physically handicapped pupil

    A. is provided with books on his exact reading level
    B. follows his own interests in selecting books
    C. is provided with good guiding questions for reading selections
    D. is required to write a report on each book he reads

5. The terms *seeking, self-selection,* and *pacing* are basic to teaching reading through the

    A. story method
    B. basal reader approach
    C. experience method
    D. individualized reading approach

6. While reading orally, a homebound child says *now-here* for *nowhere* and *all-one* for *alone.*
    Errors such as these indicate that the child shows

A. insufficient knowledge of the diphthongs
B. too little reliance on structural analysis
C. too little reliance on context clues
D. insufficient ability to blend sounds

7. Of the following, which type of sound is the EASIEST for beginning readers to discriminate? _____ sounds.

    A. Final consonant
    B. Initial consonant
    C. Short vowel
    D. Initial digraph

8. Of the following disabilities, the one MOST likely to require a body cast is

    A. muscular dystrophy
    B. scoliosis
    C. esophagitis
    D. torticollis

9. Which one of the following groups encompasses the LARGEST number of children? _____ children.

    A. Malnourished
    B. Crippled
    C. Cardiac
    D. Tuberculous

10. Rickets, a disease of nutrition manifested by disturbances in the general health and in the bones and joints, is caused by a lack of vitamin

    A. A
    B. B
    C. C
    D. D

11. Rheumatic fever

    A. most often strikes children between the ages of nine and ten
    B. is generally thought to be a streptococcal infection
    C. is generally accompanied by pain in the region of the heart
    D. is contagious

12. A young girl in your health conservation class has to have a blood transfusion every two weeks.
    She PROBABLY is suffering from

    A. gastritis
    B. hepatitis
    C. nephritis
    D. Cooley's disease

13. Differential diagnosis is MOST difficult in distinguishing between cases of

    A. poliomyelitis and meningitis
    B. aphasia and brain damage
    C. spasticity and athetosis
    D. leukemia and anemia

14. Of the following, the MOST difficult problem faced by the school in meeting the needs of the handicapped is

    A. educating the public about the potentialities of the handicapped
    B. preparing a curriculum
    C. dealing with the large number of cases that can make virtually no progress
    D. meeting the financial costs of a good educational program

15. In teaching a fourth year physically handicapped child to proofread his spelling errors in written expression, the teacher should place MOST emphasis on   15.____

    A. underlining the incorrect word
    B. writing the correct spelling in the margin
    C. checking doubtful words in a spelling list or dictionary
    D. developing the meaning of correction symbols

16. John shows a weakness in auditory discrimination of sounds. The teacher should give him practice in   16.____

    A. writing rhyming words
    B. exaggerating sounds of letters
    C. matching words with explanatory phrases
    D. listening for rhyming words

17. To help children make an effective transition from manuscript to cursive writing, the teacher should   17.____

    A. provide many examples of the same item written in both cursive and manuscript style
    B. encourage the child to write every word he sees in cursive writing
    C. explain that the difference between manuscript and cursive writing is that *in manuscript we lift the pencil*
    D. limit her chalkboard demonstration lessons to cursive writing in order to speed up the transition

18. Which of the following is a poor reading readiness activity for physically handicapped children?   18.____

    A. Story telling by the teacher
    B. Simple dramatizations by children
    C. Labelling of objects around the room
    D. Having children do exercises in a workbook

19. In teaching English to a physically handicapped non-English-speaking child, the teacher should plan to   19.____

    A. speak very slowly and more loudly than usual
    B. speak in isolated words as much as possible at first
    C. imitate the sounds and intonations of the child to facilitate early learning
    D. teach certain vowel and consonant sounds

20. In teaching mathematics to physically handicapped children in grade three, addition and subtraction facts should be drilled through   20.____

    A. relationships   B. tables
    C. experiences   D. the use of materials

21. In teaching fourth grade physically handicapped children addition and subtraction, it is BEST for them to   21.____

    A. compute all sums and differences without estimating
    B. estimate all sums and differences before computing

C. review the tables before computing
D. review *double and near doubles* before estimating

22. Which one of the following types of cerebral palsy is characterized by uncontrolled movements, facial contortions, and drooling?

    A. Ataxia   B. Spasticity
    C. Athetosis   D. Rigidity

23. Alfred Binet's PRIMARY objective in developing his intelligence test was to

    A. identify mentally retarded children in the public schools
    B. develop an effective tool for identifying the non-educable child
    C. establish norms for the general population
    D. differentiate the ament from the dement

24. The *new* mental hygiene approach to disabilities gave great impetus to the establishment of special educational facilities for the physically handicapped during the years

    A. 1866 - 1900   B. 1901 - 1918
    C. 1919 - 1950   D. 1951 - 1960

25. Improvement of conditions in the care and treatment of the orthopedically handicapped FIRST began to appear in the _____ century.

    A. 14th   B. 16th   C. 18th   D. 20th

26. Of the following, the person BEST known as an author in the area of vocational rehabilitation and job placement of the physically handicapped is

    A. Viscardi   B. Sarason   C. Frampton   D. Barker

27. Two authors who are outstanding for their writings on the psychology of the physically handicapped are

    A. Frampton and Passow   B. Ingram and Tredgold
    C. Witty and Terman   D. Barker and Wright

28. Recent advances in medical science have resulted in

    A. an overall reduction of special education facilities
    B. considerable change in the nature of the disabilities found in the special education population
    C. a more static population in terms of mobility between and among special education facilities
    D. the virtual elimination of congenital deformities

29. Which one of the following individuals did pioneer work in the field of rehabilitation of orthopedically handicapped children?

    A. Brownell   B. Deaver   C. Bakwin   D. Greenfeld

30. The PRIMARY reason for encouraging parents of physically handicapped children to participate actively in the parents' organization of their children's school is to

    A. provide them with a normal outlet away from home
    B. help them develop an understanding of the curriculum of the school
    C. foster an awareness that they are parents of children rather than of physically handicapped children
    D. permit them to develop friendships among the parents of their children's friends

---

KEY (CORRECT ANSWERS)

1.	B	16.	D
2.	C	17.	A
3.	B	18.	D
4.	B	19.	D
5.	D	20.	A
6.	C	21.	B
7.	B	22.	C
8.	B	23.	A
9.	A	24.	C
10.	D	25.	C
11.	B	26.	A
12.	D	27.	D
13.	B	28.	B
14.	A	29.	B
15.	C	30.	C

EXAMINATION SECTION
TEST 1

DIRECTIONS: Each question or incomplete statement is followed by several suggested answers or completions. Select the one that BEST answers the question or completes the statement. *PRINT THE LETTER OF THE CORRECT ANSWER IN THE SPACE AT THE RIGHT.*

1. Which of the following processes is basic to all learning? 1.____

    A. Verbalization
    B. Insight
    C. Trial and error
    D. Discrimination

2. Modern psychological theory suggests that the success of a classroom learning experience will depend PRIMARILY upon the 2.____

    A. motivation of the learner
    B. climate of the classroom
    C. readiness of the learner
    D. personality of the teacher

3. Research has demonstrated that the MOST efficient way of distributing one's effort in learning 3.____

    A. entails scheduling long units of practice with short intervals between units
    B. involves scheduling short units of practice with long intervals between units
    C. calls for units of practice and intervals of approximately equal duration
    D. depends on the material to be learned and the individual learner

4. As defined by the Gestalt psychologist, *insight* should be looked upon as 4.____

    A. a subconscious solution of a problem
    B. a sudden reorganization of experience
    C. a form of creative inspiration
    D. orientation of the learner toward the solution of a problem

5. The use of rewards and punishments to stimulate learning involves the psychological principle known as the law of 5.____

    A. effect
    B. elimination
    C. disinhibition
    D. behavioral facilitation

6. Which of the following generalizations concerning transfer of training would be accepted by MOST present-day psychologists? 6.____

    A. Positive transfer is widespread, but it is more specific than general.
    B. Little transfer occurs, but when it does, it is more or less general.
    C. There is practically no transfer from school subjects to daily living.
    D. The humanities contribute more to general improvement of thinking than mathematics or science.

7. Usually, the rate of forgetting material learned in the classroom 7.____

    A. is slow for a short time and then increases rapidly
    B. increases gradually from the time learning occurs

29

C. is rapid immediately after learning occurs and then tends to level off
D. varies depending upon the nature of the material learned

8. Peter maintains that *every one else in my class thinks I'm a crook.*
The mechanism of adjustment Peter is probably utilizing is USUALLY referred to as

   A. projection
   B. rationalization
   C. compensation
   D. identification

9. Of the following, the BEST means of helping a child develop tolerance for tension is to

   A. protect the child from experiencing frustration
   B. make the child face reality through frequent experience of failure
   C. make sure that the child is uniformly successful
   D. help the child achieve some success and face some failure

10. Phil always develops a headache when he is called upon to complete a difficult task. Phil's headache is a(n)

    A. hysteroid reaction
    B. compensatory reaction
    C. reaction formation
    D. paranoid reaction

11. Which of the following is characteristic of the person who overcompensates?

    A. Projection
    B. Repression
    C. Self-repudiation
    D. Rationalization

12. A child who has been rejected by his parents tries to *show off* at every opportunity. Such a child is USUALLY

    A. unaware of the nature of his frustration
    B. not capable of reacting more effectively
    C. reacting objectively to his stress situation
    D. deliberately trying to show his parents his need for affection

13. In former years, all members of the family of a child with a communicable disease were quarantined.
At the present time, the child's siblings may attend school unless the disease in question is

    A. diphtheria
    B. whooping cough
    C. mumps
    D. ringworm

14. The CHIEF purpose of the Snellen test is

    A. diagnosis
    B. screening
    C. placement
    D. prognosis

15. During the daily health observation period, the teacher notices that a child has evidence of pediculosis.
The teacher should

    A. isolate the child from the group
    B. send for a parent and explain the seriousness of the situation
    C. give a talk on the subject to the class
    D. refer the child to the principal for possible exclusion

16. A test designed to measure the pupil's ability to use an index, to interpret maps, and to use references would ordinarily be termed a

    A. test of general educational development
    B. diagnostic test
    C. test of work-study skills
    D. classification test

17. The twenty-fifth percentile is also known as the

    A. interquartile   B. first quartile
    C. second decile   D. quarter centile

18. George has an IQ of 96; Joe has an IQ of 104.
    Which of the following inferences can a teacher draw from these data?

    A. Joe will get higher marks in school.
    B. Joe's true IQ is probably higher than George's.
    C. Both George and Joe probably function at about the same level.
    D. The chances are even that George is really brighter than Joe.

19. The major weakness of MOST projective tests now available for use with children is

    A. their inadequate normative data
    B. their lack of usefulness with below average children
    C. the ease with which the child can fake his responses
    D. the difficulty of developing rapport with the child.

20. Correctly considered, the mental age of a child is an indication of his

    A. performance level   B. rate of mental development
    C. level of mental maturity D. aptitude level

21. A teacher of the physically handicapped plans to combine her teaching of social studies and language arts.
    This approach is

    A. *justifiable* because it saves instructional time that can be given to other areas
    B. *not justifiable* because it fails to provide for individual differences
    C. *justifiable* because it provides for learning in more meaningful situations
    D. *not justifiable* because it leads to excessive written work

22. A teacher of physically handicapped children can BEST integrate the teaching of spelling with her program of written expression by

    A. asking the children to write a sentence for each new spelling word
    B. having the children refer to a spelling list or dictionary when proofreading their written work
    C. correcting the spelling of the children's written work
    D. having the children write their misspelled words five times each for homework

23. Which of the following is the MOST important trait to be developed in a character training program for physically handicapped pupils?

    A. Respect for authority
    B. Ability to accept criticism

C. Self-discipline
D. The ability to lead and follow

24. Of the following, which is the MOST desirable criterion in selecting pictures for teaching the young physically handicapped children?

    A. Use of bright colors
    B. Strong black and white contrasts
    C. Suitable mounting and backing
    D. Artistic excellence

25. A device helpful to the physically handicapped child in developing concepts such as $8 \div 4$ and $12 - 3$ is the

    A. bar graph
    B. number line
    C. whirling wheel
    D. hygroscope

KEY (CORRECT ANSWERS)

1. D	11. C
2. C	12. A
3. D	13. A
4. B	14. B
5. A	15. D
6. A	16. C
7. C	17. B
8. A	18. C
9. D	19. A
10. A	20. C

21. C
22. B
23. C
24. A
25. B

TEST 2

DIRECTIONS: Each question or incomplete statement is followed by several suggested answers or completions. Select the one that BEST answers the question or completes the statement. *PRINT THE LETTER OF THE CORRECT ANSWER IN THE SPACE AT THE RIGHT.*

1. Research indicates that handicapped pupils, as a group, show   1._____

   A. a higher incidence of below average intelligence than the normal
   B. an IQ distribution that is skewed towards the upper end of the scale
   C. a concentration of IQ's at both extremes
   D. an IQ distribution that approximates the normal

2. According to Strauss and Lehtinen, rote serial counting should be discouraged with the brain-injured child because of his tendency toward   2._____

   A. perseveration   B. distractibility
   C. perceptual disturbances   D. hyperactivity

3. In general, children suffering from epilepsy should receive   3._____

   A. no psychological help if their seizures are adequately controlled by medication
   B. intensive psychological help, regardless of seizure control
   C. psychological help *only* in instances where neurosurgery is indicated
   D. some type of psychological help in the form of psychotherapy, guidance, or counseling

4. Which one of the following diseases may result in brain damage?   4._____

   A. Poliomyelitis   B. Lymphadenoma
   C. Spondylitis   D. Encephalitis

5. A disease USUALLY characterized by frequent vomiting and cramps is   5._____

   A. colitis   B. bronchitis
   C. myocarditis   D. empyemia

6. A lateral curvature of the spine is characteristic of   6._____

   A. scoliosis   B. lordosis   C. hyphosis   D. stenosis

7. Which of the following is one of the great dangers of many forms of anemia?   7._____

   A. Brain deterioration   B. Secondary infection
   C. Mental deficiency   D. Bleeding

8. A cleft of the vertebral column with meningeal protrusion is characteristic of   8._____

   A. Sprengel's deformity   B. scoliosis
   C. coxa vara   D. spina bifida

9. When correctly used, the term *allergen* refers to   9._____

   A. a person who is allergic
   B. an antihistamine medication
   C. a substance which produces allergy
   D. the tendency to inherit an allergy

10. Which of the following is congenital? 10._____

    A. Meningitis B. Gastro-enteritis
    C. Chronic bronchitis D. Osteogenesis imperfecta

11. Spasm is a common characteristic of 11._____

    A. slipped epiphysis B. otitis
    C. muscular dystrophy D. asthma

12. Which one of the following involves the degeneration of parts of the brain, or spinal chord, or both? 12._____

    A. Schizophrenia B. Spina bifida
    C. Multiple sclerosis D. Pott's disease

13. Of the following, the disability with the BEST prognosis is 13._____

    A. Cooley's anemia B. encephalitis
    C. hemophilia D. slipped epiphyses

14. Infectious mononucleosis is also known as 14._____

    A. Hodgkin's disease B. glandular fever
    C. chorea D. bronchiectasis

15. Which one of the following is non-inflammatory? 15._____

    A. Cystitis   B. Nephritis   C. Nephrosis   D. Pyelitis

16. Idiopathic epilepsy may be BEST characterized as a condition which 16._____

    A. is of unknown origin
    B. is a result of some trauma
    C. is not amenable to treatment
    D. may be safely ignored

17. Which one of the following conditions is characterized by loss of weight, sleeplessness, irritability, and bulging eyes? 17._____

    A. Tuberculosis B. Overactive thyroid
    C. Myasthenia gravis D. Fredericks ataxia

18. Cardiac involvement may result from a previous acute, infectious disease. The disease referred to is 18._____

    A. streptococcus sore throat B. measles
    C. uremia D. enteric fever

19. A type of facial paralysis due to a neuritis of the facial nerve in the Fallopian canal is called 19._____

    A. Paget's disease B. Bell's palsy
    C. endocarditis D. encephalitis

20. A slipped epiphysis occurs MOST frequently in 20._____

    A. early adolescence B. late adolescence
    C. pre-adolescence D. early childhood

21. An electroencephalogram would NOT ordinarily be used in connection with 21.____

    A. epilepsy B. ataxia C. peylitis D. meningitis

22. Which of the following is characterized by lifeless muscle? 22.____

    A. Pott's disease B. Flaccid paralysis
    C. Scoliosis D. Colitis

23. The psychologist's report on a child states that he suffers from aphasia. 23.____
    Aphasia is a(n)

    A. impairment of the ability to use or understand spoken language
    B. disturbance of muscular coordination
    C. neurotic reaction characterized by intense fear
    D. inability consciously to recall events or personal identity

24. *Self-education* of children, accompanied by special emphasis on the training of senses, 24.____
    is MOST closely associated with

    A. Strauss B. Cruickshank
    C. Montessori D. Lehtinen

25. In the education of physically handicapped children, current theory favors stressing the 25.____
    child's

    A. special interests B. motor abilities
    C. kinaesthetic sense D. potentialities

KEY (CORRECT ANSWERS)

1.	A	11.	D
2.	A	12.	C
3.	D	13.	D
4.	D	14.	B
5.	A	15.	C
6.	A	16.	A
7.	B	17.	B
8.	D	18.	A
9.	C	19.	B
10.	D	20.	A

21. C
22. B
23. A
24. C
25. D

TEST 3

DIRECTIONS: Each question or incomplete statement is followed by several suggested answers or completions. Select the one that BEST answers the question or completes the statement. *PRINT THE LETTER OF THE CORRECT ANSWER IN THE SPACE AT THE RIGHT.*

1. Which one of the following is MOST likely to be associated with production of large quantities of mucous?

    A. Kyphosis
    B. Bronchiectasis
    C. Lymphodenoma
    D. Thyroid deficiency

    1._____

2. Poor bladder control is MOST frequently associated with

    A. rheumatic fever
    B. hemophilia
    C. club foot
    D. torticollis

    2._____

3. Excessive accumulation of cerebrospinal fluid within the skull is USUALLY characterized as

    A. mongolism
    B. microcephaly
    C. macrocephaly
    D. hydrocephaly

    3._____

4. Cerebral palsy is a term applied to a group of conditions having in common

    A. hereditary malformation
    B. retarded mentality
    C. microcephalic appearance
    D. disorders of muscular control

    4._____

5. Which one of the following conditions is caused by the inflammation of the lower part of the intestine?

    A. Pyelitis
    B. Transverse myelitis
    C. Regional ileitis
    D. Hepatitis

    5._____

6. In contrast with former treatment methods that called for intra-muscular injections, oral medication is now frequently provided for treating

    A. diabetes   B. colitis   C. thyroiditis   D. myelitis

    6._____

7. A child who has cerebral palsy has difficulty in keeping his paper on his desk. Which one of the following materials should his teacher provide to help him?

    A. A thick piece of oaktag
    B. A paper weight
    C. Masking tape
    D. A set of tacks

    7._____

8. A bone fracture which is in the process of healing will call for greater intake of

    A. vitamin B complex
    B. folic acid
    C. vitamins D and C
    D. vitamins A and K

    8._____

9. Antihistamines are often used in treating

    A. allergies
    B. anemias
    C. glandular fevers
    D. adrenal hemorrhages

    9._____

36

10. A cardiac child classified as 4E would be MOST apt to

    A. be placed in a health conservation class
    B. receive home instruction
    C. be placed in a regular class with limited physical activity
    D. be placed in a regular class following a short stay in a special class

11. An underweight child with a cardiac condition should be encouraged to

    A. add candy to his diet
    B. add carbohydrates such as bread and milk desserts to his diet
    C. maintain weight below norm since this insures a margin of safety should illness occur
    D. increase his intake of fluids and salt

12. Joseph, a twelve-year-old boy with muscular dystrophy, is eager to do art work but cannot hold a brush or pencil in his hand.
    His teacher should

    A. help him to understand through a trial and error approach that it may be unrealistic for him to attempt art work
    B. emphasize art appreciation by bringing in copies of great paintings and discuss them
    C. encourage him to persevere until he develops the ability to hold a brush or pencil in his hand
    D. encourage him to *paint pictures with words*

13. The more severely physically handicapped child generally can engage in only a limited range of social experiences. In attempting to overcome this difficulty, the teacher should

    A. refrain from discussing exciting places and events so that the child will feel less frustrated
    B. provide as many socializing experiences as possible of a real or vicarious nature
    C. compensate for lack of social experiences by stressing the child's academic achievement
    D. ask for parental cooperation in planning frequent social gatherings of children at the student's home

14. Which of the following diseases has yielded to chemo-therapeutic treatment in recent years?

    A. Multiple sclerosis   B. Tuberculosis
    C. Diabetes   D. Scleroderma

15. The MOST satisfactory results in the treatment of epilepsy have been obtained through the use of

    A. vitamins   B. diet   C. drugs   D. exercise

16. A physically handicapped child is enclosed in a box which enables her to stand and work. The child PROBABLY suffers from

    A. scoliosis   B. Perthe's disease
    C. spina bifida   D. cerebral palsy

17. Which one of the following is MOST apt to leave home instruction and receive placement in a regular class rather than a health conservation class?
   A child with

   A. cardiac classification IB
   B. muscular atrophy
   C. arthrogryposis
   D. nephrosis

18. The use of a board with holes and a rod as an adjunct to a teaching device suggests an adaptation of a(n)

   A. abacus
   B. flannel board
   C. typewriter
   D. marble board

19. Which one of the following would be MOST useful in teaching a brain-injured child who has a severe perceptual disorder?

   A. Bright pictures that tell a story
   B. Basal readers
   C. Educational games that teach addition and subtraction facts
   D. Three-dimensional manipulative objects

20. In working with children with cerebral palsy who have problems in learning to read because of perceptual difficulties, the teacher should

   A. point to the words so that the pupil can follow the text more readily
   B. emphasize oral reading
   C. use a plain card to guide the pupil from line to line as he reads
   D. remove the neighboring children so that they offer no distractions

21. A teacher of physically handicapped children is planning a series of lessons designed to increase her pupils' vocabulary.
    Which of the following methods of introducing new words to her children will probably be MOST effective?

   A. Teaching pairs of synonyms and antonyms
   B. Teaching prefixes, suffixes, and stems
   C. Obtaining definitions of new words from the dictionary
   D. Studying the context in which the word appears

22. In teaching homonyms to handicapped children, the teacher should present

   A. them together so that the children will see the different spellings immediately
   B. each one separately, and then help the pupils to see the difference between them in use and spelling
   C. each one separately without presenting them together at any time so as to avoid confusion
   D. them in relation to antonyms and synonyms

23. John, a twelve-year-old physically handicapped child, objects to listening to radio broadcasts.
    In order to stimulate his interest MOST effectively, his teacher should

   A. prepare brief tests for him to take immediately after each broadcast
   B. permit him to read a book instead of listening

C. discuss the highlights of coming programs with him before they are heard
D. ask him to take notes during the program to be used for discussion afterwards

Questions 24-25.

DIRECTIONS: Questions 24 and 25 are based on the following situation:

The children in a special class have collected money for UNICEF. Five children brought in four cents each. One child keeps a record of collections.

24. To use this experience to develop multiplication concepts, the teacher should require that the fact be written as 24.____

    A. 5 times 4
    B. 4 times 5
    C. 5 4's
    D. 5 fours

25. To use this experience to develop measurement division, the teacher should require the children to say 25.____

    A. 20 divided by 4
    B. 20 divided by 5
    C. How many 5's in 20?
    D. How many 4's in 20?

KEY (CORRECT ANSWERS)

1.	C	11.	B
2.	A	12.	A
3.	D	13.	B
4.	D	14.	B
5.	C	15.	C
6.	A	16.	D
7.	C	17.	A
8.	C	18.	C
9.	A	19.	D
10.	B	20.	C

21.	D
22.	B
23.	C
24.	D
25.	D

EXAMINATION SECTION
TEST 1

DIRECTIONS: Each question or incomplete statement is followed by several suggested answers or completions. Select the one that BEST answers the question or completes the statement. *PRINT THE LETTER OF THE CORRECT ANSWER IN THE SPACE AT THE RIGHT.*

1. Studies of eye movements of good and poor readers indicate that the former

    A. are more aware of the details of word form
    B. space their eye movements less regularly along the line being read
    C. use more movements per line than poor readers
    D. make fewer pauses per line than poor readers

2. A characteristic of physically handicapped children is that of self-devaluation. The special class teacher can improve the situation in the MOST positive fashion by

    A. providing a series of consistently successful experiences
    B. removing from the environment those experiences which result in failure
    C. encouraging the child to rise to the occasion by meeting successfully experiences in which he has previously failed
    D. providing a series of successful experiences with an occasional failure

3. The transformation of anxiety into bodily symptoms similar to actual physical illness is USUALLY referred to as

    A. conversion hysteria
    B. a tic
    C. a phobia
    D. a compulsion

4. In using role playing as a guidance technique in a health conservation class, the teacher should

    A. write a brief play dealing with a common classroom problem for enactment by children
    B. encourage children with a problem to write a play jointly, and to act it out
    C. lead a child to solve a problem by spontaneously acting a role similar to his own personality
    D. introduce a problem about which children spontaneously act out a play

5. A child with a chronological age of eight years and a mental age of six should ordinarily

    A. be having an intensive reading readiness program
    B. not be involved in any type of reading program
    C. be able to read first grade readers
    D. be able to get the meaning of new words from context clues

6. With regard to letter writing, the specific terms *heading, salutation,* and *closing* should FIRST be taught in grades

    A. 1-2
    B. 3-4
    C. 5-6
    D. 7-8

41

7. Of the following, the CHIEF aim of language arts instruction for physically handicapped children is

    A. functional writing
    B. curricular integration
    C. recreational reading
    D. oral expression

8. The reading of maps should be taught

    A. only as an integral part of a unit of work in social studies
    B. only in specially planned lessons, apart from the unit of work
    C. both as an integral part of the unit and in special lessons planned to develop this skill
    D. as part of most lessons in social studies

9. During the period of reading readiness and the initial reading period, the physically handicapped child will be guided BEST to a recognition of words by

    A. the use of picture and context clues
    B. cutting out words from newspapers
    C. structural analysis
    D. the use of a class dictionary

10. Which one of the following procedures is of MOST value in developing problem-solving ability in grades 1-4?

    A. Children should be encouraged to solve problems in a variety of ways.
    B. Children should present problems symbolically before attempting to solve them.
    C. Most problems should be presented to children in written form.
    D. Problems presented in written form should be discussed before children attempt to solve them.

11. Research work by pupils involves each of the following skills:
    I. Organization of information to share with others Selecting most important details
    II. Locating variety of information
    III. Breaking broad problems into simpler parts

    In which sequence should the teacher of a health conservation class plan to teach these skills?

    A. I, II, III, IV
    B. IV, III, II, I
    C. II, IV, III, I
    D. III, I, II, IV

12. In grades Kindergarten through two, mathematics is taught by the teacher

    A. in a definite sequence, beginning in the first grade
    B. in a definite sequence, beginning in kindergarten
    C. in a definite sequence, beginning in the second grade
    D. as the topics arise naturally from projects in other areas or from real experiences

13. The process of *exchange* in the developmental mathematics program is encountered in examples such as

    A. 43 + 36
    B. 43 - 36
    C. 4 x 2
    D. 4 ÷ 2

14. Of the following, which is the BEST motivation for a first lesson dealing with George Washington?

    A. This picture tells me five things about George Washington. What does it tell you?
    B. I want to tell you about life in the United States in Washington's time.
    C. For homework, you were asked to read about George Washington and answer five questions about his life. Take out your homework, and let's see how well you have done.
    D. Tomorrow we shall have a test on what we learn about Washington today.

15. In the development of desirable habits of oral usage, the program for physically handicapped pupils at all elementary grade levels should stress

    A. a concern for correctness in oral communication
    B. formal instruction in grammatical elements
    C. individual practice on oral language errors
    D. formal lessons on common class errors in usage

16. In general, physically handicapped children who find it difficult to make reasonable estimates of the answers of problems before computing the answers should be

    A. permitted to disregard estimating and to compute answers to all problems
    B. given additional drill in written and computation
    C. given practice with a larger variety of problems
    D. asked to deal with problems involving simpler numbers

17. Musical toys and rhythmic instruments will have much appeal for the physically handicapped child if he FIRST

    A. uses them in group play
    B. uses them as he desires
    C. receives instruction in their use
    D. sees them played by older children

18. Personality studies of physically handicapped persons and persons not so handicapped show that

    A. there is no significant difference in frequency of personality problems between the two groups
    B. the most frequent personality deviation of the physically handicapped person is withdrawing behavior
    C. persons with closely similar disabilities tend to develop similar personality structures
    D. nearly all physically handicapped persons exhibit evidence of personality difficulties

19. The MOST common reaction of the physically handicapped child to separation from the family because of hospitalization is

    A. depression
    B. projection
    C. regression
    D. sublimation

20. Research has demonstrated that the number of epileptic seizures may be decreased through the use of psychotherapy. One may conclude from such studies that

    A. epilepsy does not involve organic brain pathology
    B. epilepsy should not be treated chemically
    C. epilepsy involves an inherent personality deformity or disorder
    D. children may react to recognizable emotional crises with hysterical convulsions

21. The wearing of braces, crutches, or casts would be apt to produce the MOST anxiety among children between the ages of

    A. 4-6   B. 7-9   C. 10-12   D. 13-15

22. Psychologists generally agree that when an emotional handicap exists in a person who has a physical disability, the emotional handicap

    A. usually stems directly from the physical handicap
    B. is usually much the same in all persons with that particular disability
    C. does not stem directly from the disability but has been mediated by social variables
    D. is apt to be extremely severe

23. According to Strauss, brain-injured retardates

    A. have a good attention span
    B. have a poorer vocabulary than the familial retardate
    C. seem to be attracted to the details of an object rather than the whole
    D. go from one task to the next with little effort

24. Which one of the following factors is MOST often cited as being deleterious to the job success of the cerebral palsied young adult?

    A. Parental overprotection
    B. Limited range of suitable occupations
    C. Difficulty of analyzing the vocational potential of the cerebral palsied
    D. Difficulty of measuring the mental ability of the cerebral palsied

25. The ability of physically handicapped individuals to cope satisfactorily with ridicule and other difficult situations

    A. depends largely on the attitudes of society toward the handicapped
    B. may be strengthened by special training in social techniques
    C. decreases as the handicapped individual matures
    D. is a function of the sex of the individual

KEY (CORRECT ANSWERS)

1.	D	11.	B
2.	D	12.	A
3.	A	13.	B
4.	D	14.	A
5.	A	15.	A
6.	B	16.	D
7.	D	17.	B
8.	C	18.	B
9.	A	19.	C
10.	A	20.	D

21. D
22. C
23. C
24. A
25. B

TEST 2

DIRECTIONS: Each question or incomplete statement is followed by several suggested answers or completions. Select the one that BEST answers the question or completes the statement. *PRINT THE LETTER OF THE CORRECT ANSWER IN THE SPACE AT THE RIGHT.*

1. In counselling cardiac students on vocational plans, which of the following would be the MOST important basis for making recommendations?   1.___

    A. Parent goals for the child's career as revealed in a teacher-parent interview
    B. Functional and therapeutic classification of the child's cardiac condition by the physician
    C. Specific individual recommendations by the physician
    D. Number of job opportunities existing in the fields suitable to the child's activity restrictions

2. For the severely physically disabled child, a realistic self-appraisal will facilitate adult adjustment.   2.___
   To foster such appraisal and adjustment, it is BEST to

    A. isolate the child with others who are similarly disabled
    B. let the child initiate his own social contacts with his peers
    C. limit the child's experiences to as few groups as possible
    D. expose the child to a variety of experiences and people

3. Children who have disabilities, as a group, tend to have more frequent and more severe psychological problems than others.   3.___
   This statement

    A. is false because most studies refute it
    B. is false because most disabled children tend to accept their disability and set lower goals for themselves
    C. is true because disabled persons are often placed in a position where they must strive for unattainable goals
    D. has not yet been substantiated because no research has been done specifically on this problem

4. Studies of children who are well-adjusted both at home and at school suggest that their good adjustment may be attributed, in large part, to   4.___

    A. favorable socioeconomic conditions
    B. the small size of their families
    C. the above average educational background of their parents
    D. parents who exhibit attitudes of understanding and acceptance

5. The following are four types of reaction of physically handicapped children to various situations: 5.___
    I. Hysteria
    II. Regression
    III. Aggression
    IV. Attention seeking
   Which two of these reactions are MOST closely related?

    A. I and IV   B. II and IV   C. III and IV   D. I and II

6. Questions directed to professionals by parents of physically handicapped children MOST frequently deal with the area of

   A. methods of care and treatment
   B. institutionalization
   C. relationship of child to other persons
   D. causation

7. John, a physically handicapped boy, has an IQ of 85 and, according to the teacher, is working up to his potential in reading. The mother, however, feels that the boy could do better work if he were given more difficult material. She requests that the teacher reveal John's IQ and reading test scores.
   The teacher should

   A. explain that the parent will not be able to understand or interpret the IQ and reading test scores
   B. show the parents the test scores and explain them to her
   C. explain that it is school policy not to show test scores
   D. suggest that the parent present her request to the principal

8. The rate of forgetting of information acquired by rote memorization is

   A. gradually accelerating
   B. gradually decelerating
   C. slow at first and then more rapid
   D. rapid at first and then slower

9. In the guidance of pupil learning, research has indicated that

   A. emphasis on correct responses is more effective than emphasis on errors
   B. demonstration is more effective than practice
   C. massed practice is more effective than distributed practice
   D. verbal guidance is more effective than demonstration

10. In considering the facilitation of learning, psychologists who utilize a field theory approach would minimize the role played by

    A. development of relationships
    B. insight
    C. learning by wholes
    D. formation of S-R bonds

11. In which one of the following areas does conditioning play a major role?

    A. Development of motor skills
    B. Acquisition of facts
    C. Development of attitudes
    D. Formation of concepts

12. Most present-day psychologists accept the principle that drill should be used in the modern classroom only when

    A. reviewing material that has already been covered
    B. it is necessary to clarify pupil understanding of a concept
    C. test results reveal poor mastery of factual material
    D. an automatic response is considered desirable

13. Of the following, which would ordinarily be the LEAST effective means of modifying an attitude?

    A. Listening to a lecture
    B. Role playing
    C. A panel discussion following a film
    D. Group discussion

14. Large print reading materials and large charts are likely to be profitably employed for children with

    A. ataxia   B. multiple sclerosis
    C. ileitis   D. hemophilia

15. In order to prevent dropped wrists or uncontrolled wrists from inordinately striking the space bar of a typewriter, it is BEST to

    A. use a cover with holes above each key of the machine
    B. use a dowel for striking the keys
    C. have the typewriter rest in a sunken area into which it fits snugly
    D. bind the wrists to produce immobility

Questions 16-21.

DIRECTIONS: Questions 16 through 21 are based on the following situation:

Norman is a fourteen-year-old boy with cerebral palsy. His vision is impaired, and he wears glasses with thick lenses. Norman has difficulty in writing because he keeps dropping his pencil. Miss Brown, his teacher, finds that he has difficulty in following the sequence of lines in the material he is asked to read. Norman also drools on his paper and speaks on inspiration. He is unsure of himself, even when it is obvious that he knows the answers to questions.

16. As a FIRST step in helping Norman with his problem in writing, Miss Brown should

    A. report the nature of Norman's writing problem to his physician
    B. provide Norman with exercises using clay in order to improve his digital dexterity
    C. tie Norman's pencil to his desk
    D. obtain the aid of a physiotherapist

17. In developing a long-range program for helping Norman solve his writing problem, Miss Brown should plan to

    A. obtain suggestions from Norman's physician concerning steps to be taken
    B. introduce Norman to the use of the typewriter
    C. ask the Bureau for the Education of the Physically Handicapped to provide a specialist to help Norman
    D. develop a series of manual exercises designed to improve digital dexterity

18. In order to help Norman solve his reading problem, Miss Brown should

   A. abandon the textbook and make greater use of teacher-made material
   B. use a card to guide Norman's eye movements as he reads the text
   C. make greater use of audio-visual aids as a supplementary activity
   D. utilize a football helmet to help reduce the external stimuli distracting Norman

19. Norman, as well as his mother, is distressed by his drooling.
    Miss Brown should

   A. train Norman to swallow frequently
   B. suggest to Norman's mother that he be well-supplied with handkerchiefs
   C. when Norman is absent, explain to the mother that drooling is the nature of his handicap
   D. train Norman to tilt his head up frequently

20. In training Norman to speak on expiration, which of the following would Miss Brown find MOST useful?

   A. A diagram of the mouth and throat
   B. Records of poems recited by famous actors
   C. A tape recorder and a candle
   D. A balloon and a feather

21. Miss Brown wants to build up Norman's confidence in himself.
    Which one of the following would be MOST effective?

   A. At every opportunity, point out to Norman that he knows the answers.
   B. Provide frequent opportunities in which Norman sees that he is successful.
   C. Praise Norman at every opportunity.
   D. Give Norman responsibilities in the home situation.

22. Strauss and Lehtinen have maintained that, with brain-injured children, the form of writing that should be taught is

   A. cursive   B. manuscript
   C. block letter printing   D. colored manuscript

23. A child who takes a regular dosage of dilantin is PROBABLY suffering from

   A. hepatitis   B. epilepsy   C. nephrosis   D. hypohidrosis

24. Socializing activities are ordinarily MOST difficult to achieve for physically handicapped children with

   A. leg fracture   B. muscular dystrophy
   C. colitis   D. asthma

25. A teacher of a physically handicapped girl discovers that her pupil's arms need immobilization during certain learning activities.
    The teacher should

   A. never use an activity that requires immobilization
   B. use a sling, twister, strap, or some other material to immobilize the arms
   C. suggest exercises to the child that will lead to better control over arm movement
   D. consult the child's physician for approval and recommendations as to methods of immobilization

KEY (CORRECT ANSWERS)

1. C
2. D
3. C
4. D
5. C

6. A
7. D
8. D
9. A
10. D

11. C
12. D
13. A
14. A
15. C

16. C
17. B
18. B
19. A
20. C

21. B
22. A
23. B
24. B
25. D

TEST 3

DIRECTIONS: Each question or incomplete statement is followed by several suggested answers or completions. Select the one that BEST answers the question or completes the statement. *PRINT THE LETTER OF THE CORRECT ANSWER IN THE SPACE AT THE RIGHT.*

1. Broad spectrum antibiotics are used MAINLY for diseases caused by   1._____

   A. parasites B. allergens
   C. degenerative factors D. bacteria

2. Frank has great difficulty in holding a pencil. His teacher should   2._____

   A. excuse him from writing activities
   B. have him use paints and brushes only
   C. provide thick pencils for his use
   D. give him drill and practice in holding a pencil

3. The name Cooley is MOST closely associated with a form of   3._____

   A. anemia B. dystrophy
   C. asthma D. cerebral palsy

4. Chorea is a disease of the _____ system.   4._____

   A. digestive B. respiratory
   C. circulatory D. nervous

5. A short lapse of consciousness and a sudden momentary pause in conversation or movement is MOST suggestive of   5._____

   A. nephrosis B. autism
   C. Friedreich's ataxia D. petit mal seizure

6. Mononucleosis is an abnormal condition of the   6._____

   A. blood B. liver C. nerves D. colon

7. Increased thirst, increased urination, loss of weight, and general fatigue are common symptoms of   7._____

   A. arthrogryposis B. diabetes
   C. hepatitis D. arthritis

8. Dementia praecox is now commonly called _____ reaction.   8._____

   A. schizophrenic B. depressive
   C. manic D. obsessive

9. Which one of the following is a disease of the ear?   9._____

   A. Ostitis B. Otitis
   C. Omphalitis D. Ophthalmia

10. Glomerulonephritis is a disease of the   10._____

    A. heart B. stomach C. kidney D. larynx

11. Which one of the following is the disease that would MOST likely impair the ability to ambulate?

    A. Diabetes
    B. Colitis
    C. Bronchiectasis
    D. Spina bifida

12. The lay term *hunchback* is synonymous with

    A. kyphosis
    B. scoliosis
    C. torticollis
    D. spondylolisthesis

13. Which one of the following diseases involves a malformation of the heart?

    A. Hydrocele
    B. Tetralogy of Fallot
    C. Myasthenia gravis
    D. Lordosis

14. Of the following, the disease which would be included under the general classification *orthopedic* is

    A. lupus erythematosus
    B. lymphedema
    C. Osgood-Schlatter's
    D. opthalmospasm

15. Of the following cardiac classifications, the one the teacher would be LEAST likely to encounter is

    A. 4A
    B. 3C
    C. 4E
    D. 2C

16. Which one of the following diseases is ALWAYS congenital?

    A. Cerebral palsy
    B. Osteogenesis imperfecta
    C. Rheumatoid arthritis
    D. Pericarditis

17. Of the following, which condition represents a disturbance of the neuro-muscular system frequently accompanied by perceptual difficulties?

    A. Perthe's disease
    B. Cerebral palsy
    C. Spina bifida
    D. Talipes

18. The following symptoms are noted in a group of children: enlargement of the calf muscles, difficulty in raising arms, afflicted shoulder and face muscles, waddling gait. The children are PROBABLY suffering from

    A. spina bifida
    B. polio
    C. muscular dystrophy
    D. Perthe's disease

19. Of the following diseases, which one is hereditary?

    A. Scoliosis
    B. Osteomyelitis
    C. Hemophilia
    D. Chorea

20. In which one of the following diseases is overweight frequently a concomitant?

    A. Pott's disease
    B. Epilepsy
    C. Slipped epiphysis
    D. Coxa Vara

21. Hyperactivity is MOST apt to be observed in children who have

    A. muscular dystrophy
    B. brain damage
    C. ileitis
    D. rheumatic fever

22. Three broad categories of physical disabilities - orthopedic, cardiac, and chronic - are often used for convenience in classifying children in health conservation classes.
The group below which BEST fits into the category of *chronic* is

    A. rheumatic fever, muscular dystrophy, kyphosis
    B. nephrosis, colitis, hepatitis
    C. Friedreich's ataxia, osteomyelitis, torticollis
    D. rickets, chorea, arthogryposis

23. Congenital malformation of the brain is often associated with

    A. hydrocephaly   B. myelitis
    C. varicella   D. lupus erythematosus

24. The use of an electroencephalogram USUALLY proves most valuable in the diagnosis of

    A. epilepsy   B. osteoma   C. lordosis   D. nephritis

25. Incontinence is MOST often an accompanying symptom of

    A. spina bifida   B. lordosis
    C. Friedreich's ataxia   D. Hodgkin's disease

KEY (CORRECT ANSWERS)

1. D		11. D
2. C		12. A
3. A		13. B
4. D		14. C
5. D		15. A
6. A		16. B
7. B		17. B
8. A		18. C
9. B		19. C
10. C		20. C

21. B
22. B
23. A
24. A
25. A

EXAMINATION SECTION
TEST 1

DIRECTIONS: Each question or incomplete statement is followed by several suggested answers or completions. Select the one that BEST answers the question or completes the statement. *PRINT THE LETTER OF THE CORRECT ANSWER IN THE SPACE AT THE RIGHT.*

1. In which one of the following aspects of mathematics will a number line be of relatively LITTLE value?

    A. Roman numbers
    B. Cardinal numbers
    C. Fractions
    D. Fundamental operations

    1.____

2. In order to help a sixth grade physically handicapped pupil understand the meaning of time belts on a map of the United States of America, the teacher should develop, on the child"s level, the concept of

    A. isochronal zones
    B. planetary revolution
    C. latitude
    D. longitude

    2.____

3. Which one of the following is MOST characteristic of a child in need of remedial reading?

    A. Non-verbal intelligence tends to be lower than verbal intelligence.
    B. Visual discrimination for word forms tends to be at an average level.
    C. Listening comprehension is lower than visual or reading comprehension.
    D. Listening comprehension is higher than visual or reading comprehension.

    3.____

4. Which one of the following CORRECTLY describes the sequence to be followed in developing an art program with young physically handicapped children?

    A. Manipulative and exploratory activities; pre-planning; intuitive design; conscious design
    B. Manipulative and exploratory activities; intuitive design; conscious design; pre-planning
    C. Pre-planning; manipulative and exploratory activities; intuitive design; conscious design
    D. Pre-planning; intuitive design; manipulative and exploratory activities; conscious design

    4.____

5. Which one of the following equations illustrates the commutative principle in mathematics?

    A. (2+3)+5 = 2+(3+5)
    B. 3x6 = (3x2)+(3x4)
    C. 4+8 = 8+4
    D. 3x4x2 = (3x4)x2 = 3x(4x2)

    5.____

6. Of the following, the BEST way to develop a sense of the long ago in physically handicapped children is to

    A. have the children tell about their vacations
    B. give them a few important dates to memorize
    C. celebrate holidays such as Thanksgiving
    D. take them to museums

    6.____

7. The teacher who wishes to demonstrate to her physically handicapped pupils the subtraction of 27 from 63 CORRECTLY uses the method of

   A. borrowing
   B. decomposition
   C. grouping
   D. equal additions

8. In which one of the following areas is a pocket chart GENERALLY used?

   A. Experiential reading
   B. Manuscript writing
   C. Science
   D. Arts and crafts

9. Which one of the following should be looked upon as appropriate reading readiness skills for physically handicapped children?

   A. Tell a simple story in sequence; follow oral directions
   B. Use context clues; pronounce words correctly
   C. Find answers to questions; read street signs
   D. Reorganize rhyming words; follow written directions

10. The technique of having a physically handicapped pupil keep a list of books that he has read is desirable particularly because it

    A. helps the teacher guide him in his choice of books
    B. serves as a valuable record
    C. serves as a good motivation for further reading
    D. helps the teacher to determine the pupil's reading ability

11. When administering an informal textbook test in reading, the teacher should test for

    A. comprehension as well as word recognition
    B. word recognition only
    C. comprehension only
    D. the child's ability to read social studies books as well as readers

12. Which one of the following is the MOST important guiding principle in teaching cursive handwriting to physically handicapped pupils?

    A. All small letters should have a straight slanting downstroke.
    B. The upstrokes of the small letters should be parallel; the downstrokes should be curved.
    C. Letter size should always be uniform and proportionate.
    D. Numbers should be slightly shorter than the letter *a*.

13. In introducing the concept of addition of two two-place numbers to physically handicapped pupils, the teacher should place relatively LITTLE emphasis upon

    A. experiences
    B. the number line
    C. the algorism
    D. representative materials

14. When the teacher leads the child to associate the spelling of *piece* with such context as *piece of pie,* she is employing a(n)

    A. exemplar
    B. mnemonic
    C. paradigm
    D. unrecommended technique

15. In working with physically handicapped children, specific training in auditory discrimination should USUALLY be

   A. regarded mostly as a remedial reading aid
   B. regarded as a kindergarten-first grade readiness activity
   C. given before the introduction of the printed symbol
   D. given after the introduction of the printed symbol

16. For the physically handicapped child, the purpose of practice or drill in social studies is to

   A. perfect a skill that has been learned
   B. provide activity for the child between instructional periods
   C. afford opportunities for the parent to work with the child
   D. introduce school experiences that normal children have

17. Research concerning the use of phonics in the teaching of beginning reading indicates that

   A. the phonics approach is superior to the word approach
   B. the word approach is superior to the phonics approach
   C. there is no essential difference in the results of the word approach and the phonics approach
   D. the phonics method produces the best results with above average children, the word approach with below average children

18. Which one of the following techniques should NOT be used in teaching number concepts to brain-injured children?

   A. Using various kinds of manipulative materials
   B. Using color on teacher-prepared number cards or worksheets
   C. Setting up a play store with various objects to sell using real money
   D. Putting only that amount of work on a worksheet that the child can do successfully

19. Of the following, the physical maturation of the child is MOST dependent on

   A. genetic factors
   B. perceptual training
   C. early home experiences
   D. early school experience

20. As a device for stimulating learning, competition seems to be MOST effective when

   A. an individual tries to exceed all others in the group
   B. one class as a whole tries to exceed another class
   C. a group of older boys tries to exceed a group of older girls
   D. a group of younger boys tries to exceed a group of younger girls

21. In the development of their theory of learning, Gestalt psychologists tend to minimize the importance of

   A. integration
   B. patterning
   C. organization
   D. drill

22. The maxim *practice makes perfect* generally does NOT apply to school learning because without teacher guidance,

   A. pupil practice is too irregularly spaced to provide growth
   B. the pupil cannot evaluate his performance

C. practice becomes boring, and the pupil stops practicing
D. the pupil fixes habits that may be incorrect

23. George, a slow learner, generally retains material better than Joe, a rapid learner. It is highly probable that George   23.____

    A. is better able to concentrate than Joe
    B. is more conscientious than Joe
    C. has overlearned the material
    D. is really more gifted than Joe

24. With regard to immediate recall of learned material, how does cramming compare with slower and more deliberate learning? Cramming is ____ effective.   24.____

    A. very much more
    B. slightly more
    C. very much less
    D. slightly less

25. Of the following ninth grade physically handicapped girls, which one is probably MOST in need of guidance?   25.____

    A. Lucy, who shows no interest in boys
    B. Ruth, who strives for perfection in all her work
    C. Alice, who shows great interest in music, but only moderate interest in her other studies
    D. Ann, who spends all her free time primping

KEY (CORRECT ANSWERS)

1.	A	11.	A
2.	D	12.	C
3.	D	13.	C
4.	B	14.	B
5.	C	15.	C
6.	C	16.	A
7.	B	17.	C
8.	A	18.	C
9.	A	19.	A
10.	A	20.	A

21. D
22. D
23. C
24. D
25. B

TEST 2

DIRECTIONS: Each question or incomplete statement is followed by several suggested answers or completions. Select the one that BEST answers the question or completes the statement. *PRINT THE LETTER OF THE CORRECT ANSWER IN THE SPACE AT THE RIGHT.*

1. Of the following, the *ism* MOST characteristic of the point of view of modern American psychologists is

    A. structuralism
    B. functionalism
    C. behaviorism
    D. connectionism

    1.____

2. A test that gives essentially the same results when applied on two or more occasions is said to be

    A. statistically unbiased
    B. representative
    C. valid
    D. reliable

    2.____

3. The median is ALWAYS the same as the

    A. mode
    B. mean
    C. fifth decile
    D. fifth centile

    3.____

4. Peter and Paul have the same IQ.
   Which one of the following statements can PROPERLY be made about the two boys?

    A. Their general knowledge is approximately equal.
    B. Their level of mental maturity is approximately equal.
    C. Their raw scores on the intelligence test are approximately equal.
    D. Their rates of mental growth are approximately equal.

    4.____

5. While the anecdotal record may serve as an important source of personality data, its MAJOR weakness is that it

    A. does not include teacher opinion of a child
    B. cannot increase teacher understanding of pupil behavior
    C. may stress unfavorable and atypical behavior
    D. gives no information about a child's social relationships

    5.____

6. A physical handicap is MOST likely to be a disturbing influence to the child who is

    A. between the ages of 3 and 8
    B. between the ages of 8 and 12
    C. an adolescent
    D. a post-adolescent

    6.____

7. When Matthew was asked to read the sentence *He saw the red bed,* he repeated again and again *saw the, saw the.*
   This is an example of

    A. distractibility
    B. disorientation
    C. mixed dominance
    D. perseveration

    7.____

8. As the orthopedically handicapped child grows older,

    8.____

    A. he tends to become less introverted
    B. his psychological problems tend to become more acute
    C. his mental ability tends to improve
    D. his anxieties tend to disappear

9. A young aphasic child

    A. always understands what is said to him but cannot respond vocally
    B. always has a hearing loss in addition to his language disorder
    C. is usually mentally retarded
    D. shows many of the same characteristics and symptoms associated with deafness

10. The proportion of children with cerebral palsy who have IQ's below 70 is APPROXIMATELY

    A. 30%   B. 50%   C. 70%   D. 90%

11. Research studies have shown that, in relation to normal children, physically handicapped children are

    A. more prone to show maladaptive reactions
    B. less likely to persist in their behavioral reactions
    C. more prone to show highly severe behavioral reactions
    D. less likely to respond to the same kinds of situations

12. Guidance of pupils with physical limitations should begin

    A. on entrance to the elementary school
    B. on entrance to the junior high school
    C. in the tenth grade
    D. in the fourth grade

13. A parent of a fourth grade physically handicapped child apparently rejects the child because of his handicap. The child's teacher should

    A. ignore the situation because she has no right to interfere with child-parent relationships
    B. arrange a conference with the parent to discuss the effect of the parent's attitude
    C. give the child more attention than she does most children to make up for the home deprivation
    D. seek the assistance of the guidance counselor

14. Peggy, a brain-damaged child, is slow in correlating her speech with her ideas. To help her with this problem, the teacher should

    A. ask questions, one at a time, at a deliberate pace
    B. minimize the need for her to respond orally
    C. permit Peggy to choose responses to questions of the multiple-choice type
    D. pose a series of questions on one topic at the same time

15. A fusion operation upon the spine is often undertaken to correct

    A. pelvimetry   B. paroxysm
    C. epiphysistis   D. scoliosis

16. The treatment program for slipped epiphysis is MOST similar to the program for   16.____

    A. torticollis   B. Perthe's disease
    C. polydactylism   D. nephrosis

17. Which one of the following conditions is MOST likely to require special educational place-   17.____
    ment?
    Fracture of the

    A. ulna   B. radius   C. femur   D. scapula

18. In MOST instances, the child with epilepsy should   18.____

    A. be permitted less than the usual amount of physical activity
    B. be assigned to home instruction
    C. attend school in a regular class
    D. be placed in a special class

19. A child with cerebral palsy drools over the pages of the reader he is using.   19.____
    The teacher should

    A. ask the child's parents to defray the cost of the book
    B. rely on inexpensive consumable materials
    C. defer book reading while concentrating on eradication of the problem
    D. insert the pages of the book in a loose-leaf folder and cover them with a transparent plastic

20. For the past twenty years, the leading cause of death in children has been   20.____

    A. rheumatic fever   B. poliomyelitis
    C. cancer   D. heart disease

21. Of the following, which one is the MOST frequent cause of long-term crippling conditions   21.____
    in children?

    A. Infections   B. Congenital defects
    C. Metabolic disturbances D. Unknown causes

22. Which one of the following statements concerning rheumatic fever and heart disease is   22.____
    CORRECT?

    A. All children who have rheumatic fever will have heart disease.
    B. Some children who have had rheumatic fever will have heart disease.
    C. No children who have had rheumatic fever will have heart disease.
    D. All children with heart disease have had rheumatic fever.

23. Of the following, which orthopedic disability gives rise to special educational placement   23.____
    of the LARGEST number of children?

    A. Slipped epiphysis   B. Multiple sclerosis
    C. Lordosis   D. Otitis

24. A disease in which the muscles appear to be replaced with fatty tissue is   24.____

    A. epiphysitis   B. kyphosis
    C. muscular dystrophy D. Still's disease

25. Prolongation of the blood clotting time results from a deficiency of vitamin   25.____
    A. B_2 B. K   C. E   D. D

KEY (CORRECT ANSWERS)

1. B
2. D
3. C
4. D
5. C

6. C
7. D
8. B
9. D
10. B

11. A
12. A
13. D
14. A
15. D

16. B
17. C
18. C
19. D
20. D

21. B
22. B
23. A
24. C
25. B

TEST 3

DIRECTIONS: Each question or incomplete statement is followed by several suggested answers or completions. Select the one that BEST answers the question or completes the statement. *PRINT THE LETTER OF THE CORRECT ANSWER IN THE SPACE AT THE RIGHT.*

1. Which one of the following BEST defines *a suffix of nouns denoting a morbid condition of growth?* 1.____

    A. Oma   B. Itis   C. Osis   D. Omy

2. The formation of an artificial anus in the anterior abdominal wall or loin is known as a(n) 2.____

    A. anuria
    B. achondroplasia
    C. colostomy
    D. plastogene

3. Carpus, ethmoid, and coccyx are 3.____

    A. arteries   B. bones   C. enzymes   D. ligaments

4. Inflammation of the intestinal tract is known as 4.____

    A. enteritis
    B. hepatitis
    C. glomerulonephritis
    D. rhinitis

5. Which one of the following conditions is CORRECTLY paired with an associated disability often found as a secondary defect? 5.____

    A. Cerebral palsy - hearing defect
    B. Chorea - visual defect
    C. Perthe's disease - speech defect
    D. Torticollis - poor coordination

6. In which one of the following pairs is it MOST difficult to arrive at a differential diagnosis? 6.____

    A. Encephalitis - meningitis
    B. Aphasia - brain damage
    C. Poliomyelitis - muscular dystrophy
    D. Hydrocephalia - microcephalia

7. Abnormal brain wave discharges are MOST characteristic of 7.____

    A. diabetes
    B. epilepsy
    C. herpes
    D. Hansen's disease

8. Polyarthritis is sometimes used as a synonym for 8.____

    A. acute rheumatic fever
    B. arthrochondritis
    C. multiple sclerosis
    D. polyneuritis

9. Pfeiffer's disease, glandular fever, and infectious mononucleosis are ALL 9.____

    A. the same disease
    B. non-communicable diseases
    C. characterized by a decrease in abnormal mononuclear cells
    D. the result of an intestinal virus

63

10. Which one of the following is classified as a fissure of the brain?　　　　10._____

    A. Maxillary plexuses 　　　　B. Periphlebitis
    C. Visceral cleavage 　　　　　D. Parieto-occipital sulcus

11. Paralysis of corresponding parts on two sides of the body is known as　　11._____

    A. diplegia　　B. hemiplegia　　C. monoplegia　　D. hemiparesis

12. Muscular dystrophy is a condition in which　　　　12._____

    A. the cause is known
    B. there is apparently no hereditary transmission
    C. several members of the family are often affected in the same manner
    D. the juvenile type is rarely found in boys

13. Tachycardia is a condition of the _____ system.　　　　13._____

    A. skeletal　　　　B. endocrine
    C. circulatory　　 D. digestive

14. Which one of the following diseases involves the lymph nodes and has a poor prognosis?　　　　14._____

    A. Colitis　　　　B. Ileitis
    C. Lordosis　　　D. Hodgkin's disease

15. Of the following diseases, the one that is NOT directly attributable to a specific vitamin deficiency is　　　　15._____

    A. scurvy　　B. beriberi　　C. tularemia　　D. pellagra

16. The three bones known as the *hammer, anvil, and stirrup* are found in the human　　　　16._____

    A. nose　　B. knee　　C. ear　　D. elbow

17. Of the following body functions, the one performed by the white blood cells is　　　　17._____

    A. carrying carbon dioxide to the lungs
    B. destroying invading bacteria
    C. carrying food particles to the cells
    D. destroying old red blood corpuscles

18. Of the following, the word *dyspnea* is MOST closely associated with　　　　18._____

    A. bronchial asthma　　B. meningitis
    C. rickets　　　　　　　D. synovitis

19. A disease characterized by tonic spasms in the voluntarily moved muscles is　　　　19._____

    A. osteomyelitis　　　B. otomycosis
    C. pleuralgia　　　　 D. myotonia congenita

20. With which one of the following is the term *aura* MOST commonly associated?　　　　20._____

    A. Psycho-motor seizures　　B. Petit mal seizures
    C. Grand mal seizures　　　　D. Laryngospasm

21. Talipes valgus and talipes varus are terms that refer to

    A. postural food defects
    B. congenital hip malformations
    C. bony protrusions
    D. ailments of the bladder

22. The responsibility of New York State for the education of a physically handicapped person ceases when the individual attains the age of

    A. 16   B. 17   C. 18   D. 21

23. Which one of the following physicians is MOST closely associated with work on tuberculosis of the spine?

    A. Erb   B. Bell   C. Pott   D. Friedreich

24. A structural technique useful in teaching mathematics to the child with special learning difficulties was developed by

    A. Thorndike   B. Stern   C. Gates   D. Eads

25. In recent years, greater numbers of institutionalized, emotionally disturbed patients are being returned to the community. Needed treatment is GENERALLY provided for such persons through

    A. family therapy
    B. aftercare clinics
    C. periodic return to the institution
    D. school agencies

KEY (CORRECT ANSWERS)

1. A		11. A	
2. C		12. C	
3. B		13. C	
4. A		14. D	
5. A		15. C	
6. B		16. C	
7. B		17. B	
8. A		18. A	
9. A		19. D	
10. D		20. C	

21. A
22. D
23. C
24. B
25. B

EXAMINATION SECTION
TEST 1

DIRECTIONS: Each question or incomplete statement is followed by several suggested answers or completions. Select the one that BEST answers the question or completes the statement. *PRINT THE LETTER OF THE CORRECT ANSWER IN THE SPACE AT THE RIGHT.*

1. Of the following, the MOST important consideration for the teacher in planning her work for a class of physically handicapped children is

    A. fostering the development of good interpersonal relationships among her pupils
    B. insuring good scholastic achievement on the part of her pupils
    C. adapting her instruction to the limitations imposed by her pupils' handicaps
    D. fostering the development of good integration of her pupils and those in the regular grades

1.____

2. The teacher of a class of physically handicapped pupils should plan her program for the day with the pupils.
It is MOST important that this plan should be

    A. followed without deviation since the pupils need a structured situation
    B. entered in the teacher's plan book at the close of the day
    C. used as a tentative guide to be changed at the teacher's direction
    D. checked and evaluated at the end of the day

2.____

3. Of the following, the MOST important purpose in teacher planning is to

    A. provide a permanent record and schedule of topics to be taught
    B. make certain that all curricular areas are included
    C. make sure that the teacher gives adequate thought to the instructional program
    D. insure the proper organization and functioning of groups

3.____

4. A class enrolling physically handicapped children in grades kindergarten through grade six has been asked to participate in a science fair.
Which one of the following groups of children in the class should be expected to participate?

    A. All the children
    B. All but the kindergarten children
    C. Grades 5 and 6 only
    D. Grades 3, 4, 5, and 6 only

4.____

5. To be MOST effective, the integration of pupils in the special education class in the school would involve their participation in

    A. audio-visual squad activities
    B. student government
    C. the school orchestra
    D. school clubs

5.____

6. A special education class, enrolling children from grades three through six, has been chosen to prepare and put on an assembly program. The pupils decide that they would like to use the abilities of every child in the class.
   Of the following, the program MOST likely to accomplish the class aim is

   A. a talent show
   B. a song fest
   C. impersonations of book characters
   D. dramatization of an excursion taken by the class

6._____

7. In grouping her pupils for reading instruction, the teacher of a special education class should place in one group those children who

   A. have similar IQ's
   B. are in the same grade
   C. have similar reading needs
   D. work together amicably

7._____

8. In grouping children for academic work in a multi-grade special education class, it is BEST to use

   A. academic achievement as a chief factor
   B. homogeneous grouping based on physical disabilities
   C. homogeneous grouping based on chronological age
   D. any grouping that will produce the least amount of physical movement as groups change for various subject areas

8._____

9. After scoring the achievement tests administered to her special education class, Miss Brown finds that four pupils are non-readers, five have reading scores between 2.2 and 2.8, five have reading scores between 3.4 and 3,9, while John has an achievement score of 4.1.
   Miss Brown should

   A. place John in a fourth group by himself
   B. place John in the group with non-readers as the teacher's aide
   C. place John in the highest group and provide individual instruction for him
   D. have John concentrate on improving his oral language techniques

9._____

10. A teacher of a special education class notices that many children who formerly put on their outer clothing without help have begun to ask for assistance. The teacher should

    A. refuse to help with their clothing
    B. report the matter to their parents
    C. have them stay after class and show them that they can do it
    D. have them assist with the children who really need the help

10._____

11. Ann, a child in a special education class, participates in the Released Time Program. Although her sister calls for her, Ann is seldom ready, and her sister has to button her coat, pack her books, etc.
    The teacher should

    A. allow Ann to get ready earlier
    B. ask the sister to call for Ann earlier

11._____

3 (#1)

    C. help Ann gather her materials and get dressed
    D. ask one of the other children in the special education class to help

12. Several children in a special education class will not taste a nutritious soup that is served at lunch. Their teacher should 12.____

    A. urge the children to try the soup
    B. withhold the dessert until the soup is eaten
    C. pay no attention to their behavior since a conflict situation should be avoided
    D. insist that the soup be eaten

13. One of the boys in a special education class insists on wearing a sweater in class in spite of the teacher's request to remove it. 13.____
    She should

    A. ignore it so as to avoid embarrassment
    B. send for a parent immediately
    C. explain to the boy how and why her request is related to his health
    D. refer the case to the principal

14. A girl in a special education class has been repeatedly taking things that do not belong to her. 14.____
    The teacher should

    A. seat the girl by herself, away from the rest of the class, so as to avoid temptation
    B. call for the parent to discuss this and to get her cooperation
    C. discuss the topic of stealing with the class without mentioning the girl's name
    D. ask the girl to return the things she has taken and explain why it was wrong for her to have taken them

15. Robert's behavior in his special education class has been quite disruptive. On this day, he refuses to listen to directions, runs around the room shouting, and annoys the other pupils. 15.____
    The teacher should

    A. send Robert to the office and thus remove him from the room
    B. send for a supervisor to obtain his assistance
    C. isolate him at the rear of the room and refuse to take notice of him until he behaves properly
    D. have Robert stand in the hall outside the classroom until he quiets down

16. A basic aim in teaching a special education class games such as *Simon Says* and *Follow The Leader* is to develop 16.____

    A. skill in running   B. coordination
    C. individual skills   D. socialization

17. In the early education of the physically handicapped child, play activities are important CHIEFLY because they 17.____

    A. serve as learning situations
    B. provide a release from more formal work
    C. give the teacher an opportunity for individualized instruction
    D. may be used as a reward for good behavior

18. Of the following, which one is the LEAST important objective in a physical education program for a physically handicapped child?
Development of

    A. agility
    B. a competitive spirit
    C. motor coordination
    D. good sportsmanship

19. Of the following, which private agency has developed programs of occupational area training for physically handicapped adolescents?

    A. Division of Vocational Rehabilitation
    B. Parents Association of Physically Handicapped Children
    C. Federation of the Handicapped
    D. Muscular Dystrophy Association

20. A parent objects strongly to following the physician's recommendation that her child return to a regular class, since the child is making excellent academic progress in the special class.
In talking to the parent, the teacher should emphasize the point that

    A. the physician knows what is best for the child
    B. the child would learn more in a regular class
    C. the child may become too attached to the special class teacher
    D. insufficient socialization may result in harm to the child

21. The teacher of a class of physically handicapped children is meeting with the parent of a boy in her class.
To be MOST effective, the teacher should discuss the boy's progress in social skills and his

    A. test grades in all subject areas
    B. current intelligence quotient, reading grade, and arithmetic grade
    C. progress in reading and arithmetic since the last report
    D. present reading and arithmetic achievement as compared with his potential

22. James' mother admits to the teacher of a special education class in a parent-teacher conference that she can understand that James would be difficult to manage in school since he is a discipline problem at home.
The teacher should request the mother to

    A. have the father do more of the disciplining
    B. try to deal more firmly with James
    C. withhold privileges from James when he becomes difficult
    D. describe in greater detail how James acts at home

23. To aid the physically handicapped child to become vocationally oriented, it is MOST desirable to have him

    A. meet the normal children to discuss vocational plans
    B. become cognizant of the special guidance services offered to handicapped children
    C. visit people who are doing the work he would like to do
    D. travel to various trade schools to see their programs in operation

24. To be MOST effective, the guidance program for the physically handicapped should be   24.____

    A. begun at adolescence
    B. integrated with other teaching
    C. taught as a special subject
    D. essentially diagnostic in scope

25. Miss Jones is preparing an experience chart with the beginning readers in a class of   25.____
    physically handicapped children aged seven to nine.
    Which one of the following words will a beginning reader find MOST easy to learn?

    A. Automobile   B. Was
    C. That   D. While

26. In teaching beginning reading to a physically handicapped child, the teacher should   26.____
    present a sight word MOSTLY through

    A. picture clues   B. phonetic analysis
    C. contextual clues   D. configuration clues

27. The outlining facts in a passage helps the physically handicapped child to   27.____

    A. develop interest in recreational reading
    B. become aware of thought relationships
    C. appreciate effective expression
    D. expand his reading interests

28. A physically handicapped child at the primary grade level should be introduced to map   28.____
    study through a

    A. globe
    B. road map of the country
    C. floor map of the classroom
    D. map of the neighborhood

29. One way to help the physically handicapped child evaluate the quality of his handwriting   29.____
    is to have him

    A. keep and compare samples of his handwriting
    B. write frequently to obtain free materials
    C. display his written work on a bulletin board in class
    D. rewrite words spelled inaccurately

30. With physically handicapped children at the primary grade level, written communication   30.____
    should emphasize

    A. accuracy of form
    B. freedom of written expression
    C. recording of sentences dictated by the teacher
    D. correct spelling

31. The important aim in teaching spelling to a physically handicapped child is to guide him   31.____
    to learn to spell correctly the words he

    A. ought to know at his age   B. uses in speaking
    C. sees in his reading   D. uses in writing

32. A teacher of a special education class finds that her younger pupils use trite expressions and overwork certain adjectives in their creative writing.
The teacher should

    A. supply the children with suggested synonyms
    B. give practice exercises in synonyms
    C. give the children lists of adjectives and have the children look up synonyms for them
    D. provide the children with experiences and develop a vocabulary based on observation

33. In teaching division to handicapped children, which one of the following examples should be the LAST one taught?

    A. $2\overline{)2480}$ B. $2\overline{)1386}$ C. $2\overline{)1376}$ D. $3\overline{)6813}$

34. A physically handicapped first grade child on the readiness level is very vocal and has a vivid imagination. The teacher can BEST help this child learn to read and write by

    A. introducing the child to the reading readiness books and having her spend more time in doing readiness activities
    B. letting the child copy a story composed by the teacher
    C. having the child copy sentences from a handwriting workbook
    D. taking down the story the child dictates and reading it back to the child

35. In helping a child in a special education class learn the sound made by *ea*, it is BEST to

    A. present words containing *ea* and then elicit words containing *ea*
    B. have the child use the dictionary to build *ea* word families
    C. present a complete list of words containing *ea*
    D. find and have the child use the appropriate section in a good workbook

36. Jane, a third grade pupil in a special education class, has not learned to make reasonable estimates in mathematics problems.
As a FIRST step in helping Jane, the teacher of the special class should have Jane

    A. deal with problems involving simple operations
    B. engage in more experiences in order to understand the problem situation involved
    C. handle representative materials to demonstrate the problem situation
    D. deal with problems involving simpler numbers

37. A physically handicapped child in the third grade reveals poor coordination in his manuscript writing.
The teacher should

    A. have the child switch to cursive writing
    B. continue to help the child improve his manuscript writing
    C. give him many practice periods for longer duration in manuscript writing
    D. introduce cursive writing, but continue with manuscript writing

38. Gerald, a fifth grade physically handicapped boy, often falters when reading aloud to his teacher. He skips over words he doesn't know and substitutes other words.
His teacher should

   A. ask Gerald to re-read the passage silently several times until he can read it smoothly
   B. allow Gerald to look up the words he doesn't know in a dictionary
   C. have Gerald make a list of the words he misses and study them
   D. find a reader for Gerald that he can read with greater ease

39. In the initial stage of learning to write, physically handicapped children should

   A. be encouraged to copy words they need from large charts made by the teacher
   B. be encouraged to copy words they need from the readers
   C. be given copies of everything they intend to write
   D. copy letter forms from the manuscript charts around the classroom

40. The wise teacher helps pupils to develop judgment and make choices.
In which one of the following might physically handicapped children be asked to participate in making a decision?

   A. Setting rules of conduct during a fire drill
   B. Locating a science area in the classroom
   C. Determining the exits to be used at dismissal
   D. Establishing traffic regulations in the corridor

KEY (CORRECT ANSWERS)

1. C	11. A	21. D	31. D
2. D	12. A	22. D	32. D
3. C	13. C	23. B	33. C
4. A	14. B	24. B	34. D
5. D	15. B	25. A	35. A
6. D	16. D	26. A	36. B
7. C	17. A	27. B	37. B
8. A	18. B	28. C	38. D
9. C	19. C	29. A	39. C
10. D	20. D	30. B	40. B

TEST 2

DIRECTIONS: Each question or incomplete statement is followed by several suggested answers or completions. Select the one that BEST answers the question or completes the statement. *PRINT THE LETTER OF THE CORRECT ANSWER IN THE SPACE AT THE RIGHT.*

1. A teacher refrains from participating both during the presentation and discussion of a report given by a committee of pupils and during the evaluation of the report by the pupils. She maintains that such participation constitutes imposition of her ideas and violates acceptable democratic procedures.
   Her viewpoint is sound with regard to

   A. the report period
   B. the evaluation period
   C. both the report period and the evaluation period
   D. neither the report period nor the evaluation period

   1._____

2. The pupils in a special education class continually color or paint the same scene - a house with a chimney out of which smoke is pouring, a border of flowers, grass at the bottom, sky at the top.
   In order to encourage more creative work, the teacher should

   A. have a directed art lesson in which pupils are instructed step-by-step on how to draw something different
   B. show children pictures of things other than houses and ask them to copy them
   C. encourage pupils to engage in non-representational fingerpainting
   D. use rexographed picture outlines for children to fill in

   2._____

3. During an expressional writing period, a teacher of a special education class finds that the children make common errors in sentence structure and in punctuation. The teacher should

   A. have the children criticize and correct each other's work during the course of the lesson
   B. disregard the formal errors provided content is good since they will decrease as the children mature
   C. indicate the errors on the children's papers and have the children rewrite the papers correctly
   D. set aside definite periods for teaching correct usage in formal aspects of composition

   3._____

4. Homework assignments for handicapped children in the seventh and eighth years should require a total of NO MORE THAN _____ minutes.

   A. 30-40   B. 40-50   C. 50-60   D. 60-90

   4._____

5. A teacher of a special education class has developed a series of questions that she uses as a guide for evaluating her physical education program.
   Which one of the following questions should she answer in the NEGATIVE? Have I

   A. made provision for all pupils in the class to participate according to their interests and needs?
   B. provided for integrating physical education with the health program?

   5._____

C. emphasized group activities rather than individual skills?
D. set aside definite time in the schedule for physical education?

6. One important function of special class placement for a child with a rheumatic heart condition is to

   A. have him immobilized in a sheltered environment
   B. satisfy the parent with educational placement
   C. have him recover from his fear of physical activity
   D. make sure that he takes his medication

7. Several eleven-year-old boys in a special education class want to make ping pong paddles.
   To make such paddles, it is BEST to use

   A. balsa wood   B. oak
   C. plywood   D. fir

8. In special classes for the orthopedically handicapped child, a combination seat and desk unit is used because it

   A. reduces the amount of furniture in the room
   B. may be adjusted to the postural needs of the student
   C. gives more service than separate units
   D. permits the pupil to work independently

9. The teacher of a class of physically handicapped children decides to organize the class into groups for reading. These groups should

   A. remain fixed for the rest of the school year
   B. be subject to constant reorganization to meet pupil needs
   C. be reorganized regularly, about once a month
   D. be so organized as to have an equal number of boys and girls

10. Several children in a special education class get together and work at a common hobby. This type of group activity is

    A. *undesirable,* because it does not relate to instruction in specific skills
    B. *desirable,* because the result will be of value
    C. *undesirable,* because it is organized by the children
    D. *desirable,* because it is organized by the children

11. The teacher of a special education class will probably encounter the FEWEST disciplinary problems in a classroom where

    A. she mandates procedure, designates working groups and tasks, and carefully checks on completion of work
    B. complete freedom for group or personal decision exists
    C. she has promulgated a set of rules and regulations which she follows scrupulously
    D. rules and regulations have been developed through group discussion, with the teacher acting as a guide

3 (#2)

12. Joseph, a quiet, unaggressive eleven-year-old in a special education class, is ridiculed by his fellow pupils because he is always dirty and unkempt. The teacher has been unable to secure parental cooperation in improving his appearance.
    To deal with this situation, the teacher should

    A. through direct teaching show Joseph how to care for his personal appearance
    B. isolate Joseph in a corner of the room until he makes an effort to improve
    C. attempt to bring about a better acceptance of Joseph through a series of lessons on tolerance
    D. send Joseph home to be cleaned up each time his personal appearance does not meet an acceptable standard

    12.____

13. During her first week of teaching, a newly appointed teacher of a special education class should be MOST concerned with

    A. determining the intellectual level of her children
    B. completing the work she plans for each day
    C. grouping pupils for reading
    D. maintaining good order

    13.____

14. A teacher of a special education class has been asked to select children for a remedial reading program.
    She should give preference to those children who

    A. obtain the lowest scores on a standardized achievement test
    B. show the greatest discrepancy between mental age and reading age
    C. have demonstrated the most eagerness to learn
    D. do not present conduct problems in the classroom

    14.____

15. A teacher of a special education class presents a lesson in reading to the entire class. This approach can be defended ONLY if the teacher's aim is to

    A. develop a common basis for understanding
    B. gear instruction to the *average* child in the group
    C. encourage broad socialization
    D. save time and effort

    15.____

16. At lunch time, the teacher of a special education class finds that the children eat the soft part of their sandwiches and throw away the crusts.
    The teacher should

    A. eliminate the daily snack period
    B. give a lecture on wasting food
    C. show pictures of children in Asia searching for food
    D. start a unit on nutrition

    16.____

17. In the development of a unit on *Safety in the Street,* children in a primary special education class discuss safety workers and their jobs. The class decides to develop an experience chart as a culmination of the lesson. The MOST appropriate title and story would be

    A. OUR FRIEND, THE POLICEMAN
    B. COMMUNITY SAFETY WORKERS
    C. HELPING THE SAFETY WORKERS HELP US

    17.____

D. THE WORK OF SAFETY EXPERTS

18. In planning for an assembly program, the teacher of a special education class should   18.____

    A. have every child participate in the program
    B. use a published play to make certain that the quality is high
    C. use only the more talented children in order to make a good impression on other classes
    D. select a play that calls for colorful costumes so that skills other than dramatization will be called upon

19. Of the following, the MAJOR advantage which filmstrips possess over motion pictures as an instructional aid in special education classes is that the former   19.____

    A. are less expensive
    B. are easier to obtain
    C. are more adaptable for discussion
    D. provide a clear picture

20. Of the following, the MOST effective medium for preparing instructional wall charts for classroom display is   20.____

    A. a ballpoint pen   B. colored chalk
    C. black crayon   D. a brush pen

21. A teacher of a special education class receives a supply allotment of two gallons of turpentine and six quarts of shellac solvent. He must remove some materials from the paint closet in order to make room for the new supplies. The materials which may be safely removed from the paint closet are   21.____

    A. jars of tempera paints   B. cans of enamel paints
    C. cans of varnish   D. bottles of paint drier

22. During the daily health inspection period, the teacher of a special education class discovers a child with pediculosis.   22.____
    The PROPER procedure is to

    A. provide the child with tincture of green soap and have the child clean up the condition
    B. isolate the child until an ambulance arrives
    C. censure the child tactfully for bringing such a condition to school
    D. refer the child for possible exclusion from school

23. A teacher finds that her special education class is very noisy and disorderly when entering the room at the beginning of the school day.   23.____
    In order to correct this, she should have

    A. a monitor in charge of the class when they enter the room
    B. the children go to their seats with their clothing and remain there until she calls upon them to hang up their clothing, one at a time
    C. an assignment on the blackboard which the children are to do as soon as they have been given instructions to hang up their clothing
    D. the class line up outside the room and wait there until she brings them into the room

24. Jethro, a recent admission to your special education class located in a middle income neighborhood, is a suspected truant about whom the mother has expressed considerable concern.
    On the first day of Jethro's unexplained absence, you should

    A. call the Bureau of Attendance
    B. mail a note to the parent
    C. visit his home at noon time to determine whether the absence is legitimate
    D. telephone his home at the earliest opportunity

25. In an attempt to stimulate better work in mathematics in the class, a teacher of a special education class plans to prepare a wall chart in which the grade scores of each child will be presented graphically.
    As a motivational technique, the procedure described would be

    A. *poor,* because the role of relative capacity and effort is not taken into account
    B. *poor,* because young children cannot interpret charts and graphs
    C. *good,* because it stimulates all pupils equally
    D. *good,* because it adds an element of competition which ordinarily does not appear in such classes

26. Which of the following teachers is using the approach MOST conducive to the development of a climate of emotional security in the classroom?

    A. Teacher sends a birthday card to each child in the class.
    B. Teacher shows marked concern when the child returns to the class.
    C. After an absence, teacher makes a special effort to correct mistakes made by the child.
    D. Teacher arranges special displays and exhibits for each topic studied by the class.

27. Good discipline is MOST effectively established by the teacher of a special education class through

    A. careful planning and good teaching
    B. showing friendliness and being interesting
    C. demonstrating calmness and efficiency
    D. exercise of good judgment and lack of favoritism

28. Simon, a ten-year-old pupil in a special education class, keeps running to the teacher to show her what he is doing and waits for her approval before he returns to his desk. The teacher should

    A. give Simon all the attention that he needs
    B. involve Simon in group activities with other children
    C. tell Simon to come to the desk only when it is very necessary
    D. tell Simon that she will see him once in the morning and once in the afternoon

29. A teacher wishes to organize her class of physically handicapped children, ranging in age from nine to twelve years, into groups for more effective teaching of reading. The BEST criteria to use for such grouping are

    A. chronological age and IQ
    B. IQ and social maturity
    C. achievement level in reading and individual needs

D. social maturity and chronological age

30. Modern educators strongly favor grouping of children in various curriculum areas for teaching purposes.
    The MOST important reason for such grouping is that it

    A. makes the teacher's job easier
    B. makes it possible to work more intensively with the children
    C. makes it possible to better meet the needs of the individual child
    D. enables children to make more rapid progress

31. In teaching reading, the teacher of a special education class enrolling children in grades one to three should generally organize no more than _____ group(s).

    A. 4 B. 3 C. 2 D. 1

32. Which one of the following is the MOST important criterion to apply in judging the adequacy of a report given by a child in a special education class?

    A. Is the report presented extemporaneously, rather than read?
    B. Is the report based upon reference to more than one source?
    C. Does the report raise many new questions to be answered?
    D. Does the report reflect the work of one child or of the committee of which he is a member?

33. Marvin's behavior in his special education class has been quite disruptive. On this day, he refuses to listen to directions, runs around the room shouting, and annoys the other pupils.
    The teacher should

    A. send for a supervisor to obtain his assistance
    B. send Marvin to the office
    C. isolate him at the rear of the room and refuse to take notice of him until he behaves properly
    D. have Marvin stand in the hall outside the classroom until he quiets down

34. In using the Snellen letter chart, an *eye test line* should be marked on the floor in the classroom _____ feet from the chart.

    A. 15 B. 20 C. 25 D. 30

35. Jean, a nine-year-old pupil in a special education class, is ignored by the other children in the class.
    Her teacher should

    A. leave Jean alone and not interfere with the preferences of the other children
    B. talk about democratic procedures in class so that the children will know how she feels about the matter
    C. give Jean interesting work to do so that she won't mind being left alone
    D. involve Jean in a project that requires working with another child

36. George, an underweight child in a special education class, refuses to drink the container of milk which the school supplies because he doesn't like to drink milk.
    The MOST desirable step for the teacher to take is to

A. insist on his drinking the milk
B. tell him that he cannot eat his lunch unless he drinks his milk
C. bar him from some activity he enjoys unless he drinks his milk
D. permit him to eat lunch without milk and arrange to consult with his parents

Questions 37-39.

DIRECTIONS: Questions 37 through 39 are based on the following situation.

A special education class is planning to take a trip to a neighboring public market in connection with a unit on food.

37. In preparation for the trip, the teacher emphasizes the importance of good behavior. The reason to be stressed with the children is:

    A. People will call you stupid if you don't behave
    B. You won't be able to go back for a second visit if you don't behave
    C. You should act in such a way as to gain the respect of others
    D. You will be reported to the principal if you don't behave properly

38. In planning the trip,

    A. the teacher should ask all the children to observe carefully and to report on as many different things as they see
    B. a committee composed of a few children should be held responsible for formulating a report on the trip
    C. definite questions should be formulated before the trip is taken for the purpose of finding answers to them
    D. follow-up activities should be left to the initiative of the pupils

39. Of the following, the MOST desirable follow-up activity after the trip is to

    A. hold a discussion to answer questions or evaluate understandings
    B. make a summary of the highlights of the trip
    C. visit the public library to find books and materials concerning different kinds of foods
    D. read a book dealing with one of the countries from which the foods they have seen come

40. In discussing *Safety During Fire Drills* with her special education class, Miss Jones outlines the procedures to be followed.
The rule which applies to all fire drills at all times is:

    A. Be sure to take the same partner every time
    B. As soon as all the children have their coats on, we shall leave the room
    C. There shall be absolute silence during the fire drill
    D. Be sure that all windows are wide open before the class leaves the room

KEY (CORRECT ANSWERS)

1. D	11. D	21. A	31. B
2. C	12. A	22. D	32. C
3. D	13. D	23. C	33. A
4. D	14. B	24. D	34. B
5. C	15. A	25. A	35. D
6. C	16. D	26. A	36. D
7. C	17. A	27. A	37. C
8. B	18. A	28. B	38. C
9. B	19. C	29. C	39. A
10. D	20. D	30. C	40. C

TEST 3

DIRECTIONS: Each question or incomplete statement is followed by several suggested answers or completions. Select the one that BEST answers the question or completes the statement. *PRINT THE LETTER OF THE CORRECT ANSWER IN THE SPACE AT THE RIGHT.*

1. Which one of the following statements BEST meets the criteria for good anecdotal reporting?

    A. John is continually taking things that belong to other boys in the class. He is the biggest sneak-thief I have ever taught.
    B. This morning John started a fight with Elaine when my back was turned. You have to watch him every minute or he gets into trouble.
    C. When called on this morning, John gave an excellent answer to a difficult question. He has yet to volunteer any information in class.
    D. John always pushes the other children in the class. He is a big bully.

1.____

2. Of the following, the PRIMARY objective in administering standardized achievement tests to a class of children with physical disabilities is to

    A. diagnose deficiencies in various subject areas
    B. formulate expectancy levels for pupil performance
    C. group the class for instruction
    D. determine the standing of the class in relation to other classes in the school

2.____

3. With which of the following types of tests are the names of Strong, Kuder, Cleeton, and Lee-Thorpe associated?

    A. Intelligence tests
    B. Achievement batteries
    C. Reading readiness measures
    D. Interest inventories

3.____

4. There is a wealth of evidence to indicate that, for large random samples of children, intelligence level is MOST significantly related to

    A. socio-economic level of the family
    B. racial origin
    C. national origin
    D. ordinal position in the family

4.____

5. A teacher of a special education class develops a socio-gram for her group. Which one of the following questions is MOST likely to be answered through analysis of the socio-gram?

    A. What kind of handicap tends to isolate a child?
    B. Is there a strong possibility that class spirit is lacking?
    C. Which children are sought out by others because of the high academic achievement?
    D. Which child has strongly aggressive tendencies?

5.____

6. In which one of the following instances will fifty percent of a group be below the median for the group?

6.____

A. Always regardless of the distribution
B. When the distribution is bimodal
C. When the mean and median coincide
D. Only when the distribution is skewed

7. George, who cheats on examinations whenever he has an opportunity to do so, always claims that his classmates try to copy his answers to test questions,
George is utilizing the mechanism of adjustment known as

A. projection B. sublimation
C. compensation D. identification

8. Mrs. Green has scheduled a series of individual conferences with parents of children in her special education class, Mrs. Green should plan to close each conference

A. on an optimistic note
B. by summarizing her plans for the pupil
C. by indicating what the parent can do to help
D. by discussing what the pupil must do to improve

9. The parents of the children in a special education class have not participated in school activities because they are sensitive and feel that the other parents in the school are not faced with problems similar to theirs.
The teacher should suggest that

A. they form a Mother's Club of their own, apart from P.T.A.
B. they join the P.T.A., attend their meetings, and serve on some of their committees
C. the principal organize special workshops for the parents of the special education class only
D. the class activities in which they participate are sufficient and adequate and that they need not participate in any others

10. Philip is a recent admission to a special education class. In arranging to confer with his parents, the teacher's BEST approach would be to

A. visit the home while Philip is away so that matters may be discussed freely
B. invite the parents to visit the class during the school day
C. visit the home the first time Philip misbehaves
D. make an appointment with the parents before visiting the home

11. Which one of the following is MOST desirable as part of the special equipment for a class of severely orthopedically handicapped children?

A. Sewing machine B. Electric page turner
C. Electric drill D. Anatomical models

12. The teacher of a special education class notices that a child with rheumatic heart disease is reluctant to end the rest period and resume lessons. The child says he is tired.
The teacher should

A. speak to the child about the importance of resuming lessons and encourage him to do so more promptly
B. extend the child's rest period
C. have the child resume work but make sure that the work is of a sedentary nature

D. consult with the parent to ascertain possible reasons for the child's behavior

13. The MAJOR activity of philanthropic organizations servicing physically handicapped children has been in the area of

    A. providing additional funds for instructional materials
    B. offering scholarship incentives
    C. offering opportunities for vocational exploration
    D. providing opportunities for socialization

14. Which one of the following groups of children has been taught in schools rather than at home with increasing frequency in recent years?
Children with

    A. diabetes
    B. nephrosis
    C. epilepsy
    D. cystic fibrosis

15. In teaching social studies to a special education class, the teacher should

    A. avoid the use of the unit method because of varying grades and handicaps
    B. use a different unit problem for each child because of his individual needs
    C. use a different unit problem for the pupils of each grade so as to avoid repetition from grade to grade
    D. use the same unit problem for the entire class so that the children work cooperatively

16. Research on the place of phonics in reading indicates that all of the following statements are true EXCEPT:

    A. Phonics as a word recognition clue is most divorced from meaning
    B. Some children profit greatly from teaching in phonics
    C. Phonics is a good preliminary to learning to read in the initial stages
    D. Phonics teaching may begin after a child has a sight vocabulary of about 100 words

17. The philosophy underlying the educational program for physically handicappped children

    A. does not differ basically from that accepted for all children
    B. stresses the development of security for the mental retardate
    C. emphasizes specialized training in specific job areas
    D. minimizes the development of academic skills

18. Recent research in the area of school learning has demonstrated that

    A. the pupil who learns most rapidly generally shows poor retention
    B. the stimulation provided by a group approach to a learning situation generally leads to more effective learning
    C. blame is as effective as praise in increasing pupil learning
    D. distribution of practice has little effect in determining the degree of pupil mastery

19. Of the following, the MOST important factor determining the retention of arithmetic concepts by elementary school children is the

    A. distribution of learning periods
    B. motivation of the learner

C. meaningful and realistic application of the concepts learned
D. use of the concepts in areas other than arithmetic

20. The book entitled THE PSYCHOLOGY OF THE PHYSICALLY HANDICAPPED was written by

    A. Fouracre
    B. Lee and Lee
    C. Gall
    D. Pintner et.al.

21. The educational and psychological difficulties of brain-injured children are discussed in a book by

    A. Hamilton
    B. Strauss and Lehtinen
    C. Gates
    D. Axline

22. In which of the following are the contributing authorities CORRECTLY matched with the area of work indicated?

    A. Epilepsy - Lennox, Putnam
    B. Cardiovascular diseases - White, Cruickshank
    C. Rehabilitation - Salk, Deaver
    D. Cerebral palsy - Phelps, De La Chapelle

23. Mary's mother comes hurriedly into the playground explaining that she is late for Mary's clinic appointment and asks that Mary be excused at once.
    The teacher should

    A. permit Mary to leave with her mother
    B. send the mother to the office for a written authorization
    C. send Mary to the office with her mother
    D. ask a colleague to cover the class and take Mary and her mother to the office

24. An irate mother of a boy in a special education class claims that the bus driver is always *fresh* to her son, John.
    Of the following, the BEST immediate statement for the teacher to make to the mother is:

    A. Wait and we will speak to the driver together
    B. I will report this to the bus company at once
    C. John has been quite difficult in school lately
    D. I will look into this and get in touch with you

25. Some parents of children in a special education class complain that their children are not getting the same program as the other pupils in the school.
    The teacher should explain that

    A. their children's mental health is more important than their studies
    B. the basic curriculum is changed or modified for other children in the school, depending on need
    C. the same curriculum is followed by all the pupils in the school
    D. their children are not ready physically or psychologically for the same school program as the other pupils

26. During the time set aside for parent-teacher interviews, it is MOST desirable for the teacher to

A. carry on a group interview with three or four parents
B. invite parents to observe pupils at work
C. arrange for a private interview with each parent
D. visit the homes of several parents

27. A mother of one of the girls in a special education class refuses to permit her child to go on a trip with the class because she is overprotective and fearful of her safety. The teacher should

    A. leave the child with one of the teachers in the school
    B. invite the parent to accompany her child so that she can be reassured of her safety
    C. invite the parent to join some of the other parents in accompanying the class so that they may assist the teacher
    D. reassure the parent that she will keep the child close to her throughout the entire trip so that she can give her personal attention

28. As a means of meeting the needs of the physically limited child, the after-school recreational programs of community agencies are

    A. *recommended,* because they help develop useful graded skills
    B. *not recommended,* because they remove the child from the security of his home
    C. *recommended,* because they help develop social interaction and self-dependence
    D. *not recommended* because they generally stress overly competitive activities

29. Which one of the following disabilities is apt to require the MOST special precautionary measures on the part of the health class teacher?

    A. Pragilitas ossium   B. Syndactylism
    C. Rheumatic fever   D. Arthritis

30. In a class for brain-injured children, the teacher should plan to provide

    A. colorful room decorations
    B. attention-getting bulletin board picture displays
    C. multi-colored curtains
    D. as few displays and decorations as possible

31. Of the following, which is the BEST way of extending an invitation to a mother for a conference?

    A. Extend an oral invitation to the mother by telephone
    B. Send a sealed note home with the child
    C. Schedule a group parent-teacher meeting
    D. Mail a letter to the mother asking her to attend

32. Montesaori boards are used MOST frequently with children who are

    A. cardiac   B. epileptic
    C. tuberculous   D. orthopedically handicapped

33. Which one of the following is MOST likely to be part of the special classroom equipment for severely handicapped orthopedic pupils?

    A. Audio-visual aids   B. Overhead bars
    C. Canvas mats   D. Hydraulic desks

34. Bursitis, spondylitis, myositis, and sciatica are diseases which are often included under the more general term

    A. thrombosis
    B. rheumatism
    C. arthritis
    D. myxedema

35. An essential difference between nephrosis is that nephritis

    A. is a kidney disease; nephrosis is a disease of the liver
    B. may occur at any age; nephrosis occurs only in adulthood
    C. suggests the presence of an inflammation; nephrosis occurs without signs of inflammation
    D. is relatively rare in frequency of occurrence; nephrosis occurs much more frequently

36. New programs for physically handicapped children in school settings have frequently been introduced following successful pilot projects conducted by

    A. parent groups
    B. research organizations
    C. private welfare agencies
    D. public health agencies

37. Workers in the field of special education have recently shown a revival of interest in the methods originally developed for use with young children by

    A. Pestalozzi
    B. Binet
    C. Froebel
    D. Montessori

38. In recent years, considerable progress has been made in the out-patient treatment of the emotionally disturbed individual through the use of

    A. prefrontal lobotomy
    B. chemotherapy
    C. shock treatment
    D. hydrotherapy

39. Recent research by the Division of Vocational Rehabilitation has been directed to the exploration of the effectiveness of pre-vocational guidance for the physically handicapped student within the age group of _____ and _____ years.

    A. 6; 9   B. 10; 13   C. 14; 16   D. 17; 20

40. At the federal level, provision for school programs concerning exceptional children is MAINLY the responsibility of the

    A. Department of the Interior
    B. Department of Health, Education, and Welfare
    C. Federal Security Agency
    D. Department of Labor

KEY (CORRECT ANSWERS)

1. C	11. B	21. B	31. D
2. C	12. D	22. A	32. D
3. D	13. D	23. B	33. B
4. A	14. C	24. B	34. C
5. B	15. C	25. B	35. C
6. A	16. C	26. C	36. A
7. A	17. A	27. C	37. D
8. A	18. B	28. C	38. B
9. B	19. C	29. C	39. C
10. B	20. D	30. D	40. B

EXAMINATION SECTION
TEST 1

DIRECTIONS: Each question or incomplete statement is followed by several suggested answers or completions. Select the one the BEST answers the question or completes the statement. *PRINT THE LETTER OF THE CORRECT ANSWER IN THE SPACE AT THE RIGHT.*

1. Students with hearing impairments are likely to have IEP goals in the area(s) of
    I. speechreading
    II. using amplification devices
    III. sign language
    IV. mobility

    A. I and II
    B. I, II and III
    C. III and IV
    D. I, II, III and IV

1.____

2. Which of the following is a type of systematic observation?

    A. Time sampling
    B. Anecdotal recording
    C. Duration recording
    D. Internal recording

2.____

3. The basic teaching procedure that typically proves most successful with preschool-aged mentally retarded students is

    A. using advanced organizers
    B. targeting sequential skills for instruction
    C. overlearning
    D. focusing on activities of daily living

3.____

4. Which of the following words refers specifically to a disability in spelling?

    A. Dysphonia
    B. Dysgraphia
    C. Dyslexia
    D. Dysorthography

4.____

5. If a student or parents wish to file a complaint against an agency or institution for violation of the Family Educational Rights and Privacy Act (FERPA), the complaint must be filed within _____ days of the date of the alleged violation, or from the date that the complainant knew or reasonably should have known of the alleged violation.

    A. 45
    B. 90
    C. 180
    D. 360

5.____

6. A child writes the word "bog" instead of "dog." This is an example of

   A. dysorthography
   B. proactive inhibition
   C. word-attack
   D. static reversal

7. Each of the following is a guideline to be used in assisting hearing-impaired students in their vocabulary development, except

   A. aural, followed by printed or written presentations, should be presented
   B. the vocabulary should be presented in a consistent context
   C. new vocabulary should have a concrete purpose for the child
   D. new vocabulary should be constantly presented

8. The _____ technique for determining readability involves the use of 150-word passages of continuous writing in which every fifth word is omitted.

   A. miscue
   B. Flesch
   C. cloze
   D. System Fore

9. Each of the following is a problem associated with an autosomal recessive gene, except

   A. Down syndrome
   B. Tay Sachs disease
   C. Hurler syndrome
   D. Phenylketonuria

10. Which of the following is a hard neurological sign?

    A. Impulsivity
    B. Perceptual problems
    C. Expressive aphasia
    D. Incoordination

11. Which of the following is a paralinguistic mechanism?

    A. Rate of delivery
    B. Body and head posture
    C. Facial expression
    D. Proxemics

12. Curriculum in the Brolin model focuses on each of the following areas, except

    A. daily living skills
    B. occupational guidance and preparation
    C. academic and linguistic skills
    D. personal-social skills

13. If the parents of a disabled child disagree with any provision of a proposed individual instruction plan, they can request a due process hearing and a review from   13.____

    A. the school administration
    B. the district board
    C. the state educational agency
    D. the federal Department of Education's Office of Civil Rights (OCR)

14. Approximately what percentage of students with learning disabilities are regarded as having language-learning disabilities?   14.____

    A. 20-35
    B. 40-60
    C. 50-75
    D. 80-95

15. Which of the following concepts refers to the alertness or adaptability of a person that exists independently of education and experience?   15.____

    A. Innate set
    B. Fluid intelligence
    C. Modality
    D. Operant behavior

16. In terms of special education, a person's "developmental period" is usually considered to be between the ages of   16.____

    A. 0 and 15
    B. 3 and 16
    C. 0 and 18
    D. 3 and 25

17. The main disadvantage associated with using Renzuli's rating scale as a screening device for gifted/talented programs is that it   17.____

    A. focuses inordinately on IQ
    B. is relatively time-consuming
    C. provides no cutoffs
    D. is limited in scope

18. Which of the following are homophenes?   18.____

    A. *c* and *e*
    B. *b* and *m*
    C. *v* and *w*
    D. *t* and *s*

19. Which of the following skills is least likely to be included in a self-control curriculum?   19.____

    A. Motor coordination
    B. Relaxation
    C. Sequencing and ordering
    D. Memory

20. In order to be protected under the federal regulations regarding discrimination in education, a disabled person's physical or mental impairment must have a substantial limitation on _____ or more major life activities such as seeing, hearing, learning, etc.

    A. 1
    B. 2
    C. 3
    D. 4

21. A student is consistently having problems in math computation, specifically in the area of carrying. For example, the student solves a problem in the following way:

    $$\begin{array}{r} 76 \\ +66 \\ \hline 1312 \end{array}$$

    The student also frequently acts out in class. The teacher of this student would be advised to

    A. initiate a formal assessment by the school's special education team
    B. refer the child to a learning specialist
    C. administer a brief inventory of mathematical abilities, to diagnose any other problem areas
    D. take the student aside and teach him the specific rule about carrying digits, and then observe him for a while.

22. Which of the following is a process assessment?

    A. Rorschach Inkblot Test
    B. Burks Behavior Rating Scales
    C. Stanford Binet Intelligence Test (SB)
    D. Frostig Test of Visual Perception (DTVP)

23. The most significant language characteristic of hearing-impaired children has to do with their

    A. morphology
    B. syntax
    C. spelling
    D. vocabulary

24. When reading, a student perceives individual symbols, but is unable to recognize them as part of a whole word. This is an example of visual

    A. indiscrimination
    B. agnosia
    C. dyslogia
    D. aphasia

25. A terminally ill child will generally go through a series of stages in his or her way toward accepting the inevitability of death. Which of the following is typically experienced first?

    A. Resentment
    B. Psychosomatic symptoms

C. Resistance of usual routine
D. Guilt feelings

26. Generally, the most widely-used form of assessment for determining the need for special education services is

   A. norm-referenced testing
   B. observation
   C. curriculum-based assessment
   D. criterion-referenced testing

27. A child is asked to recognize the letter *d* immediately following the presentation of the letter *b*, but the prior learning of *b* causes some confusion.
This is an example of

   A. proactive inhibition
   B. dysorthography
   C. retroactive inhibition
   D. dyslexia

28. The academic/basic skills approach for teaching mildly to moderately retarded students

   A. emphasizes reading and math skills
   B. emphasizes compensatory skill development in younger students
   C. emphasizes remedial skill development in older students
   D. is used primarily to develop memory and the "how-to-learn" process

29. Which of the following behaviors is least likely to be exhibited by a student who has suffered a traumatic brain injury?

   A. Impulsivity
   B. Overestimation of abilities/bragging
   C. Sleep disorders
   D. Social withdrawal

30. Pacers commonly used as instructional aids in reading programs include each of the following, except

   A. place markers
   B. films
   C. switches
   D. blinkers

31. Which of the following tests does not include a measure of reading comprehension?

   A. Iowa Test of Basic Skills (ITBS)
   B. Peabody Individual Achievement Test–Revised (PIAT-R)
   C. Wide Range Achievement Test 3 (WRAT3)
   D. Stanford Achievement Test (SAT)

32. Language disorders include
    I. difficulty in producing speech sounds
    II. the improper use of speech sounds
    III. dysfluency
    IV. the improper use of words

    A. I only
    B. I and II
    C. II and IV
    D. III only

33. Oralism is a method of teaching that involves each of the following, except

    A. writing
    B. speechreading
    C. fingerspelling
    D. auditory training

34. A child with no prior classroom problems is thin and listless, and frequently needs to visit the restroom. The classroom teacher should be on the lookout for further signs of

    A. phenylketonuria
    B. rheumatic fever
    C. diabetes
    D. leukemia

35. The ruling of the *Larry P. v. Riles* case in 1972 was that

    A. intelligence tests were banned throughout the state of California
    B. standardized testing was considered biased against black and disadvantaged students
    C. all further assessments in the state of Arizona were to be nonbiased against disadvantaged students
    D. schools were required to deliver "related services," such as catheterization for a student with spina bifida

36. The legal qualification concerning the ability of one to understand the nature and effect of one's acts is

    A. adequacy
    B. competence
    C. lucidity
    D. capacity

37. Which of the following conditions is generally LEAST prevalent among students who require special education services?

    A. Emotional disturbance
    B. Mental retardation
    C. Visual impairment
    D. Learning disability

38. Which of the following terms is usually identified with the work of Wolfensberger?

    A. Socialization
    B. Normalization
    C. Mainstreaming
    D. Habilitation

39. A classroom teacher can help a student with a stuttering problem by

    A. cutting short a difficult speech attempt and moving on to something else
    B. calling on children randomly, rather than in rows or alphabetically, for oral responses
    C. reacting with sympathy to an episode of stuttering
    D. adopting a more authoritarian control of the classroom

40. The Movigenics learning program stresses perceptual-motor training, especially in the _____ area.

    A. tactile
    B. visual
    C. olfactory
    D. auditory

41. A child complains of headaches and nausea after doing close work that involved reading and drawing. The first thing a classroom teacher should suspect is

    A. a complex partial seizure
    B. a vision impairment
    C. a generalized absence (petit mal) seizure
    D. diabetes

42. Which of the following is/are likely to help decrease the incidence of a child's dysfluency in a classroom setting?
    I. Singing
    II. Speaking in monotone
    III. Whispering
    IV. Reading aloud to the class

    A. I and II
    B. I, II and III
    C. III and IV
    D. I, II, III and IV

43. What is the collective term for teaching strategies based on the assumption that students will learn more efficiently if the teaching is geared toward specific, clearly identified learning strengths and weaknesses of the student?

    A. Occupational therapy (OT)
    B. Individually prescribed instruction (IPI)
    C. VAKT technique
    D. Aptitude-treatment interactions (ATI)

44. Which of the following is a system of recording observation data in which the number of times a behavior occurs is noted?

   A. Event recording
   B. Time sampling
   C. Duration recording
   D. Internal recording

45. Which of the following historical figures in the field of special education is credited with coining the term "special education"?

   A. Grace Femald
   B. William Cruickshank
   C. Samuel Kirk
   D. Marianne Frostig

46. One example of an affricate is the

   A. *j* sound in *jump*
   B. *p* sound in *stop*
   C. *z* sound in *zoo*
   D. *l* sound in *follow*

47. A classroom teacher who works with a child on grammatical constructions is teaching

   A. pragmatics
   B. phonology
   C. semantics
   D. syntax

48. The decision-making element that is essential to all effective adaptive behavior is

   A. id control
   B. executive decision
   C. screening
   D. batch processing

49. Which of the following terms refers to a person's acting in an inhibited manner?

   A. Neurasthenic
   B. Lalophobic
   C. Kolytic
   D. Catatonic

50. A student in the classroom is observed to breathe continually through her mouth, and seems to be persistently inattentive to classroom activities. The teacher should begin to suspect that this student may

   A. have a metabolic disorder
   B. be asthmatic
   C. be experiencing complex partial seizures
   D. have a hearing problem

KEY (CORRECT ANSWERS)

1. B	11. A	21. D	31. C	41. B
2. A	12. C	22. D	32. C	42. B
3. B	13. C	23. D	33. C	43. D
4. D	14. B	24. B	34. C	44. A
5. C	15. B	25. B	35. A	45. C
6. D	16. C	26. B	36. D	46. A
7. B	17. C	27. A	37. C	47. D
8. C	18. B	28. A	38. B	48. B
9. A	19. A	29. D	39. B	49. C
10. C	20. A	30. C	40. B	50. D

TEST 2

DIRECTIONS: Each question or incomplete statement is followed by several suggested answers or completions. Select the one the BEST answers the question or completes the statement. *PRINT THE LETTER OF THE CORRECT ANSWER IN THE SPACE AT THE RIGHT.*

1. Special education is typically regarded as having four components. Which of the following is not one of these?   1.____

    A. Social milieu
    B. Use of equipment
    C. Physical environment
    D. Teaching procedures

2. Which of the following items of federal legislation provides for the awarding of attorney's fees and costs to parents who are successful in litigation regarding special education discrimination?   2.____

    A. Rehabilitation Act of 1973
    B. Handicapped Children's Protection Act of 1986
    C. Individuals with Disabilities Education Act (IDEA), as amended
    D. Americans with Disabilities Act (ADA) of 1990

3. Students with physical impairments are considered to be particularly disadvantaged when it comes to the taking of _____ tests, because of their restricted ability to explore the world around them.   3.____

    A. criterion-referenced
    B. projective
    C. norm-referenced
    D. process

4. Which of the following is a form of aphasia?   4.____

    A. dyscalculia
    B. agraphia
    C. alexia
    D. akinesia

5. Which of the following is a projective assessment?   5.____

    A. Woodcock Reading Mastery Test
    B. Stanford Achievement Test (SAT)
    C. Thematic Apperception Test (TAT)
    D. Basic School Skills Inventory (BSSI)

6. For the purposes of determining school compliance with federal legislation, the factors used in determining whether a person's impairment substantially limits a major life activity include the impairment's   6.____

    I. duration
    II. observable manifestations
    III. nature and severity
    IV. permanent or long-term impact

A. I and II
B. I and IV
C. I, III and IV
D. I, II, III and IV

7. A child begins her learning of the word *impossible* by learning that the meaning of the prefix *im-* is, roughly, "not." This is an example of

    A. the whole word method
    B. structural analysis
    C. truncation
    D. phonics

8. Which of the following is a scale used to assess respondents' attitudes toward a particular issue, item, or situation?

    A. Lincoln-Ozoretzky
    B. Barraga
    C. Vineland
    D. Likert

9. In ensuring accessibility for all students, a school's physical plant should have doors with openings of at least _____ inches wide.

    A. 24
    B. 32
    C. 48
    D. 55

10. By definition, in order to be considered mentally retarded, a person must have
    I. poor communicative ability
    II. low-measured intelligence
    III. deficits in adaptive behavior

    A. I and II
    B. II only
    C. II and III
    D. I, II and III

11. Articulation disorders are considered to be the most common of all speech disorders among school-age students, and include each of the following types, <u>except</u>

    A. omissions
    B. distortions
    C. elisions
    D. substitutions

12. Which of the following terms is used to describe activities that are designed to increase an individual's awareness of his or her body in space and its movement through different planes?

    A. Proprioceptive
    B. Kinetic

C. Efferent
D. Vestibular

13. Which of the following is a type of prosthesis?

    A. Obturator
    B. Kernicturus
    C. Dyad
    D. Shunt

14. If curriculum-based assessments are used for determining the needs of an exceptional student, it is recommended that a student be administered at least _____ different tests on different occasions to ensure that the student has or has not mastered the content.

    A. 2
    B. 3
    C. 4
    D. 5

15. Which of the following terms is different in meaning from the others?

    A. Operant learning
    B. Incidental learning
    C. Inferential learning
    D. Informal learning

16. Each of the following is an approach to creating an environment that should be used by teachers of preschool-aged mentally retarded students, except

    A. allowing for occasional intervals of unstructured time
    B. providing programmed teacher absences from activities and interactions
    C. arranging different areas of the classroom in different ways, in order to signal different expectations
    D. establishing routines to classroom instruction

17. Any information collected about a behavior before an intervention is implemented is defined as _____ data.

    A. control
    B. threshold
    C. blind
    D. baseline

18. Which of the following is a legal term referring to a competent person who, although not appointed a guardian, acts in behalf of a party who is unable to look after his or her own interests?

    A. Trustee
    B. Warden
    C. Conservator
    D. Next friend

19. Behavior that is learned and is therefore under an individual's control is described as _____ behavior.

    A. crystallized
    B. operant
    C. discriminating
    D. fluid

20. Which of the following would be an element of organic therapy?

    A. Drugs
    B. Rewards/tokens
    C. Norm-referenced tests
    D. Movigenics

21. Which of the following methods for teaching deaf students combines the oral method and finger spelling?

    A. Clark
    B. Kinesthetic
    C. Rochester
    D. Oral-aural

22. In most cases, a parent or eligible student must provide a signed and dated written consent before an educational agency or institution may disclose personally identifiable information from the student's educational records. This prior consent would be required when the disclosure is

    A. in connection with financial aid for which the student has applied
    B. to state educational authorities
    C. to other school officials within the agency or institution whom the agency or institution has determined to have legitimate educational interests
    D. to the parents of a disabled child other than the child whose records are requested, for the purpose of determining the agency's or institution's compliance with federal regulations

23. A curricula principle used with severely and profoundly handicapped students is the _____ principle.

    A. Peter
    B. partial participation
    C. psychometric
    D. Premack

24. What type of instruction is preferable when teaching students with severe or profound mental retardation?

    A. Individualized
    B. Peer/mentor tutoring
    C. Small group
    D. Large classroom

25. Which of the following sounds is considered to be a plosive?

    A. m
    B. s
    C. l
    D. g

26. Which of the following types of tests is an assessment of a person's prevocational and career skills?

    A. Brigance
    B. Weschler
    C. Stanford Binet
    D. Woodcock-Johnson

27. When mental retardation is suspected, a team typically meets to prepare an assessment plan. During this meeting it is generally considered important to collect information about at least three areas of current performance. Which of the following is not one of these areas?

    A. Sensorimotor ability
    B. Academic achievement
    C. Adaptive behavior
    D. Intellectual functioning

28. A special education assessment for a child who is suspected of having a sensory impairment would include a determination of
    I. developmental status
    II. academic achievement
    III. communicative status
    IV. intellectual functioning

    A. I and II
    B. II, III and IV
    C. III, only
    D. I, II, III and IV

29. The definition of a legally blind person includes those whose field of vision is restricted to an angle of _____ degrees or less.

    A. 10
    B. 20
    C. 30
    D. 45

30. Each of the following sounds is typically distorted in a lateral lisp, except

    A. s
    B. ch
    C. v
    D. j

31. Each of the following is a classroom adaptation that should be helpful to a student with a vision impairment, except

    A. providing a large desk surface
    B. using a flexible seating arrangement for different activities
    C. seating the student directly facing a window
    D. providing easels and adjustable desktops

32. When communication disorders are suspected in a student, it is most important to first

    A. assign primary assessment responsibility to the speech-language pathologist
    B. maintain written parental consent for assessment
    C. administer a standardized measure such as the Goldman-Fristoe Test of Articulation
    D. check the student's hearing

33. Which of the following historical figures in the field of special education was actively involved in developing remedial reading techniques?

    A. Eduoard Seguin
    B. Grace Fernald
    C. Maria Montessori
    D. Samuel Gridley Howe

34. An 8-year-old child is considered to have a mental age of 6 and a grade age of 1. What is the child's expectancy age?

    A. 3
    B. 5
    C. 7
    D. 8

35. A classroom teacher works with a child on the development of vocabulary. This is an example of instruction in the area of

    A. pragmatics
    B. morphology
    C. semantics
    D. syntax

36. Which of the following statements, concerning a teacher's knowledge about a student's physical or health problem, is generally false?

    A. There is no justifiable reason for grouping children according to their medical diagnoses
    B. Only a minority of children with physical or health problems have any special education needs at all
    C. The names of the medical conditions experienced by the child will be the deciding factor in deciding the student's individual special education needs
    D. The most important factor in forming an appropriate learning environment for most students is mobility

37. Common uses of a sociogram include each of the following, except

   A. modification of classroom relationships
   B. diagnosing the social perception of individuals
   C. screening purposes
   D. determining the social position of class members

38. Dialect differences are often a cause of _____ speech disorders.

   A. resonatory
   B. prosodic
   C. articulation
   D. phonatory

39. Overall, approximately _____% of the school-aged population in the United States are considered "exceptional" (including handicapped and gifted).

   A. 2-6
   B. 10-12
   C. 14-17
   D. 18-25

40. Which of the following amplification devices is generally most appropriate for people with sensorineural hearing loss?

   A. Infrared auditory trainer
   B. Hearing aid
   C. FM wireless auditory trainer
   D. Cochlear implant

41. According to Piaget, the first stage of cognitive development is the _____ stage.

   A. preoperational
   B. formal operations
   C. sensorimotor
   D. concrete operations

42. As a rule, adaptations required in teaching procedures for physically impaired students involve three aspects, the first of which is

   A. computer instruction
   B. accommodation
   C. teaching toward independence
   D. task analysis

43. Which of the following teaching procedures is most appropriate for mentally retarded students in an elementary classroom?

   A. overcorrection
   B. one-on-one instruction
   C. community-based instruction
   D. advanced organizers

44. The areas of instruction in the Clark model of career education for the handicapped include each of the following, except   44._____

    A. human relationships
    B. health and wellness
    C. values, attitudes, and habits
    D. job and daily living skills

45. Which of the following is a visual disorder that is considered to be an accommodation problem?   45._____

    A. Amblyopia
    B. Astigmatism
    C. Nystagmus
    D. Esophoria

46. Disadvantages of the "enrichment triad" curriculum approach for gifted students include each of the following, except   46._____

    A. resource-intensiveness
    B. it ignores the relationship between gifted and regular programs
    C. difficulties in assessing creativity and task commitment
    D. it is relatively new and unresearched

47. The degree to which individual scores, subtests, or performance items vary from one another on a particular test is known as   47._____

    A. scatter
    B. scope
    C. distribution
    D. range

48. Which of the following is a resonance process speech disorder?   48._____

    A. Abnormal pitch
    B. Cluttering
    C. Breathiness
    D. Hypernasality

49. The measure of how well the items of a given test sample the subject matter or situation about which conclusions can be drawn is known as _____ validity.   49._____

    A. content
    B. predictive
    C. construct
    D. concurrent

50. The adapted communication system preferred for preschool-age deaf children is generally   50.____
    A. cued speech
    B. the aural-oral method
    C. the Rochester method
    D. American sign language (ASL)

KEY (CORRECT ANSWERS)

1. A	11. C	21. C	31. C	41. C
2. B	12. D	22. D	32. D	42. D
3. C	13. A	23. B	33. B	43. D
4. C	14. B	24. C	34. B	44. B
5. C	15. A	25. C	35. C	45. B
6. C	16. A	26. A	36. C	46. B
7. B	17. D	27. A	37. B	47. A
8. D	18. D	28. B	38. A	48. D
9. B	19. B	29. B	39. C	49. A
10. C	20. A	30. C	40. D	50. D

EXAMINATION SECTION
TEST 1

DIRECTIONS: Each question or incomplete statement is followed by several suggested answers or completions. Select the one the BEST answers the question or completes the statement. *PRINT THE LETTER OF THE CORRECT ANSWER IN THE SPACE AT THE RIGHT.*

1. In the context of special education, what is a term that refers to the number of exceptional children who exist at any given time?

    A. Frequency
    B. Prevalence
    C. Scope
    D. Incidence

    1._____

2. Which of the following types of assessments is typically used to make eligibility decisions regarding special education services?

    A. norm-referenced testing
    B. observation
    C. curriculum-based assessment
    D. criterion-referenced testing

    2._____

3. What is the term for the inability to perform mathematical functions especially the inability to manipulate arithmetic symbols or do simple mathematical calculations?

    A. Incomputence
    B. Dyscalculia
    C. Immathematica
    D. Acalculia

    3._____

4. Which of the following terms, referring to a method of teaching reading, is different in meaning from the others?

    A. Whole word
    B. Look-say
    C. Phonic
    D. Sight

    4._____

5. For a student with a communication disorder, the classroom teacher's most important responsibility is to

    A. develop the student's individualized education program
    B. encourage the student's participation and ensuring that his/her attempts at oral communication are accepted with tolerance and support
    C. target the skills that need to be reinforced in the classroom
    D. make major environmental adaptations to accommodate the student

    5._____

6. Which of the following forms of mental retardation is considered to constitute 75% or more of those identified as mentally retarded?

    A. Clinical
    B. Relative

    6._____

C. Pharmacological
D. Psychosocial

7. In general, the handicapping condition which receives the largest percentage of an educational agency's special education services is

    A. learning disability
    B. speech impairment
    C. emotional disturbance
    D. mental retardation

8. Under federal law, school districts are responsible for evaluating at public expense all students suspected of having disabilities from birth through _____ years of age.

    A. 16
    B. 18
    C. 21
    D. 25

9. In a normal test-score distribution, approximately _____% of the scores will fall within the limits of one standard deviation above and below the mean.

    A. 24
    B. 46
    C. 68
    D. 87

10. The major approach to the education of mainstreamed students with mild retardation is

    A. conceptualization
    B. thematic instruction
    C. pragmatics
    D. habilitation

11. The term "agitolalia" refers to

    A. the total loss of ability to receive, associate, and understand visual language symbols
    B. very rapid and cluttered speech due to stress or other emotional problems
    C. an inability to recognize and identify familiar objects through a particular sense organ even though the receiving organ itself is not impaired
    D. the inability to recall kinesthetic writing patterns

12. Which of the following is an achievement test that is typically administered individually, in cases of assessment for special needs?

    A. Stanford Achievement Test (SAT)
    B. Metropolitan Achievement Test (MAT)
    C. Kaufman Test of Educational Achievement (K-TEA)
    D. Iowa Test of Basic Skills (ITBS)

13. Which of the following is a perinatal cause of mental retardation?

A. Lead poisoning
B. Nutritional defects
C. Fetal alcohol syndrome
D. Prematurity

14. The measure of how well test scores match measures of contemporary criterion performance is known as _____ validity.

    A. face
    B. construct
    C. concurrent
    D. content

15. During classroom discussion, a student with a communication disorder asks, "May I use the westwoom?" Most of the other students have heard his misarticulation. As classroom teacher, the best response would be to

    A. say simply, "yes," and send the child to the restroom
    B. gently point out that the child has mispronounced "restroom," and ask him to try again
    C. ask another student to demonstrate the correct pronunciation of "restroom"
    D. say, "Of course you may use the restroom," and send the child on his way

16. What is the term for the process of shaping the tone quality of speech and controlling whether the sound comes through the mouth or nose?

    A. Morphology
    B. Phonation
    C. Resonance
    D. Prosody

17. Which of the following educational approaches is designed specifically to work with children with reading disabilities?

    A. Quay-Peterson
    B. Montessori
    C. Orton-Gillingham
    D. Clark

18. A "partially sighted" student is defined as one whose vision in the best eye is between _____ after the best possible correction.

    A. 20/40 and 20/100
    B. 20/70 and 20/150
    C. 20/70 and 20/200
    D. 20/100 and 20/200

19. Which of the following court cases was related to the timeliness of providing special education placement and services?

    A. PASE v. Hannon (1978)
    B. Rowley v. Board of Education (1982)
    C. Jose P. v. Ambach (1983)
    D. Irving Independent School District v. Tatro (1984)

20. Tools used to assess the visual efficiency of children with low vision include the _____ scale.

    A. Snellen
    B. Flesch
    C. Quay-Peterson
    D. Barraga

21. Which of the following terms is used to denote mental activity that does not conform to reality or logic?

    A. Syllogistic
    B. Iterative
    C. Dereistic
    D. Affective

22. Which of the following terms is generally used to denote the minimal stimulus necessary to produce a response or sensation, such as hearing?

    A. Threshold
    B. Discriminator
    C. Origin
    D. Baseline

23. In ensuring accessibility for all students, a school's physical plant should have ramps whose grade is no more than a _____-inch rise for every 12 feet of length.

    A. 1
    B. 2
    C. 4
    D. 6

24. Which of the following is a term describing the wide variety and forms of communicative behaviors that do not involve speech?

    A. Nondiscursive
    B. Nonlexical
    C. Nuncupative
    D. Rhetorical

25. Each of the following is a classroom adaptation that should be helpful to a student with a hearing impairment, except

    A. labeling items in the classroom
    B. seating the student away from noise
    C. allowing the student to move around the room when observing lectures, activities, or presentations
    D. teachers and other speakers standing with a direct light behind them

26. The major focus of the developmental-skills approach to teaching mildly mentally retarded students is

    A. attention and memory
    B. the categorization of skill domains

C. compensation for unlearned abilities
D. the development of sequential skills

27. A child who consistently utters "oat" instead of the word "coat" exhibits an articulation disorder known as 27._____

   A. substitution
   B. omission
   C. distortion
   D. ellipsis

28. Which of the following is a measure of the learning aptitude of people between the ages of 3 and 16 who are deaf? 28._____

   A. McCarthy Scales of Children's Abilities (MSCA)
   B. Pictorial Test of Intelligence (PTI)
   C. Detroit Tests of Learning Aptitude (DTLA)
   D. Nebraska Test of Learning Aptitude (NTLA)

29. A person's ability to apply past experience to a current situation is known as 29._____

   A. arbitration
   B. mediation
   C. cognition
   D. reflection

30. "Marked hearing loss" is generally defined as a _____ dB loss. 30._____

   A. 10-36
   B. 41-55
   C. 56-70
   D. 74-90

31. Legally, the term "parent" includes a 31._____
   I. legal guardian
   II. trustee
   III. temporary custodian
   IV. warden

   A. I only
   B. I and II
   C. I, II and III
   D. I, II, III and IV

32. Which of the following is a word used to describe any condition that is acquired after birth–for example, as a result of accident or illness? 32._____

   A. Incidental
   B. Adventitious
   C. Token
   D. Fortuitous

33. Which of the following is not a neuroleptic drug? 33._____

A. Thorazine
B. Ritalin
C. Haldol
D. Mellaril

34. Words not verified by concrete experiences, often used by the visually impaired, are described as

    A. verbalisms
    B. rhetoric
    C. stapes
    D. nebulae

34.____

35. Which of the following adapted communication systems involves the representation of various sounds and vowels with the hands, which are generally placed around the mouth and throat area?

    A. Total communication
    B. The oral-aural method
    C. The auditory method
    D. Cued speech

35.____

36. What is the term for the aspect of language related to meaning?

    A. Syntax
    B. Denotation
    C. Semantics
    D. Logos

36.____

37. The area of teaching content that typically receives the greatest emphasis with the majority of physically impaired students is

    A. communication and language
    B. self-care
    C. problem-solving
    D. vocational preparation

37.____

38. Which of the following is a possible sign of a language disorder?

    A. Use of the word "funner" instead of the phrase "more fun"
    B. Pronouncing the *r* sound as *w*
    C. Stuttering
    D. Persistent whispering

38.____

39. The major implication of Henry Goddard's 1914 publication of his Kallikak family study was that mental retardation was

    A. a relative term
    B. hereditary
    C. neurological in origin
    D. a cultural phenomenon

39.____

40. Which of the following training programs is essentially oriented toward visual-perceptual development?

40.____

A. Madison plan
B. Montessori method
C. SEED
D. Frostig approach

41. The use of labels in special education—for example, regarding students with a wide variety of problems and handicaps as "emotionally disturbed"—is considered to have the disadvantage of

    A. discouraging the development of advocacy agencies
    B. confusing the communication among professionals in special education
    C. excluding services from a large percentage of students
    D. making legislation and regulations regarding special education services difficult

41.____

42. The educational needs assessment of a child with a physical or health impairment should generally focus on each of the following, except

    A. adaptive behavior
    B. daily living activities
    C. academic potential
    D. psychosocial development

42.____

43. The assignment of scaled scores to a set of raw scores is done through the process of

    A. extrapolation
    B. abduction
    C. interpolation
    D. adduction

43.____

44. Which of the following screening procedures for potentially gifted/talented students provides the most subjective or troublesome-to-define results?

    A. Trained teacher's judgement
    B. Informal rating scales
    C. Creativity tests
    D. Renzuli's rating scale

44.____

45. As amended, the federal Individuals with Disabilities Education Act (IDEA) orders that the state must ensure the provision of a free and appropriate public education (FAPE) to

    A. all children from birth to 18 years of age
    B. all children from birth to 21 years of age
    C. all children between the ages of 3 and 21
    D. a student of any age who seeks an opportunity for public education

45.____

46. The language development problem most likely to occur with blind children is

    A. difficulty associating words with concepts
    B. difficulty forming certain vowel sounds
    C. delayed communication skills
    D. persistent syntax errors

46.____

47. Which of the following programs is based on building a developmental hierarchy of skills in the child, beginning with attendance?

47.____

A. Instrumental enrichment
B. Engineered classroom
C. Movigenics
D. Class meeting

48. On average, which of the following consonant sounds will take the longest for any child to master in speech?   48.____

    A. *ch*
    B. *f*
    C. *zh*
    D. *ng*

49. Which of the following types of speech disorders would be managed in the form of training compensatory production patterns for improved intelligibility?   49.____

    A. Phoneme omission
    B. Dysarthria
    C. Hyponasality
    D. Dysfluency

50. Which of the following is/are a primary indicator of mild mental retardation in a school setting?   50.____
    I. Slower rate of learning
    II. Communication disorders
    III. Developmental delays in most areas

    A. I only
    B. I and III
    C. II and III
    D. I, II and III

KEY (CORRECT ANSWERS)

1.	B	11.	B	21.	C	31.	A	41.	C
2.	A	12.	C	22.	A	32.	B	42.	A
3.	D	13.	D	23.	A	33.	B	43.	C
4.	C	14.	C	24.	A	34.	A	44.	C
5.	B	15.	D	25.	D	35.	D	45.	C
6.	D	16.	C	26.	D	36.	C	46.	A
7.	A	17.	C	27.	B	37.	A	47.	B
8.	C	18.	C	28.	D	38.	A	48.	C
9.	C	19.	C	29.	B	39.	B	49.	B
10.	D	20.	D	30.	C	40.	D	50.	B

TEST 2

DIRECTIONS: Each question or incomplete statement is followed by several suggested answers or completions. Select the one the BEST answers the question or completes the statement. *PRINT THE LETTER OF THE CORRECT ANSWER IN THE SPACE AT THE RIGHT.*

1. Which of the following is a system of observation in which the observer describes all the behaviors that occur?

    A. Narrative recording
    B. Event recording
    C. Time sampling
    D. Duration recording

    1.____

2. Which of the following adapted communication systems uses all the components of the oral-aural method and sign language?

    A. Total communication
    B. Cued speech
    C. The auditory method
    D. The Rochester method

    2.____

3. In United States history, the parents of disabled children who first filed suit against their school districts for excluding children with disabilities were prompted by the case of

    A. Brown v. Board of Education (1954)
    B. Mills v. Board of Education of the District of Columbia (1972)
    C. Board of Education v. Rowley (1982)
    D. Stauffer v. William Penn School District (1993)

    3.____

4. Which of the following is not a cognitive teaching strategy?

    A. Rehearsal training
    B. Response cost
    C. Attention training
    D. Instrumental enrichment

    4.____

5. As a curricular guideline for teaching severely or profoundly mentally retarded students, the criteria of ultimate functioning model

    A. has been questioned because of its assumption that such students can or should develop at the same rate as other students
    B. targets instructional objectives that match the student's chronological age
    C. emphasizes the use of adaptive equipment
    D. uses milestones achieved by students without handicaps as keys to what should be taught the handicapped student

    5.____

6. Before being asked to write a word from memory, a child is prompted to trace its form on the page. This is an example of the _____ method.

    A. kinesthetic
    B. oral-aural

    6.____

C. whole word
D. Movigenic

7. Which of the following teaching procedures has been recommended for both blind and partially sighted students?   7.____

   A. adapted writing techniques
   B. individual study
   C. increased time allotment for task completion
   D. color-coded instructions

8. Which of the following is a multimeasure approach to assessment that emphasizes the functional analysis of student behaviors?   8.____

   A. Time sampling
   B. Adaptive-process assessment
   C. Psycholinguistic testing
   D. Longitudinal study

9. Which of the following historical figures in the field of special education was/were among the first to suggest and research a neurological basis for learning problems?   9.____

   A. Frostig
   B. Conant
   C. Strauss and Werner
   D. Periere and Itard

10. Which of the following is a fluency disorder?   10.____

    A. Distortion
    B. Loudness
    C. Cluttering
    D. Omission

11. Generally, an IEP under federal guidelines must include each of the following, except   11.____

    A. identification of procedures and schedules for evaluating student progress toward goals and objectives
    B. identification of short-term educational objectives
    C. detailed description of a learning environment that falls under the federal definition of "least restrictive"
    D. documentation of the student's current academic performance level

12. Which of the following terms refers to the beginning signs or symptoms of a particular disorder?   12.____

    A. Prognostic
    B. Rudimentary
    C. Organic
    D. Prodromal

13. A child with no prior classroom problems is often observed by the classroom teacher to be staring straight ahead, while at the same time making chewing and swallowing movements. The teacher should consult the health personnel at the school about the possibility of

    A. diabetes
    B. epilepsy
    C. hemophilia
    D. Tourette's syndrome

14. Effective antecedent teaching procedures for mentally retarded students usually include
    I. providing verbal instructions
    II. physical demonstration or modeling
    III. color-coding certain tasks

    A. I only
    B. I and II
    C. II and III
    D. I, II, and III

15. Which of the following is a process or technique for employing rating scales in the study of the emotional meaning or attraction of words?

    A. Semantic differential
    B. Afferent lexicon
    C. Reaction formation
    D. Thematic apperception

16. A person's ability to perceive visually and identify wholes when only parts are presented--for example, recognizing a particular word after seeing only a part of the word--is known as visual

    A. fusion
    B. efficiency
    C. closure
    D. acuity

17. Therapy for young developing stutterers should generally include each of the following, except

    A. managing the child's environment
    B. behavior therapy
    C. direct speech training
    D. counseling parents and family

18. Which of the following voice disorders is characterized by things such as breathiness, hypernasality, denasality, or hoarseness?

    A. Loudness
    B. Quality
    C. Pitch
    D. Tone

19. Which of the following is a disadvantage associated with the structure-of-intellect model of curriculum for gifted programs?

    A. Associated materials are difficult to use
    B. It doesn't address the problems of gifted students who are having trouble learning
    C. It isn't a "stand-alone" approach
    D. It doesn't provide a total framework for curriculum development

20. According to the Family Educational Rights and Privacy Act of 1974, schools that receive federal funding must make student records available for viewing by parents and legal guardians, and by the students themselves, providing the student in each case is

    A. capable of proving that he or she understands the implications and intended use of the records
    B. no longer enrolled at the institution from which the records are requested
    C. 18 years of age or older
    D. not intending to use the records as the basis for a legal action against the institution from which the records are requested

21. Students who have difficulty in _____ usually experience problems if they are taught by a multisensory approach.

    A. spelling
    B. reading
    C. traducing
    D. discriminating

22. Which of the following speech peculiarities is most likely to be displayed by an autistic student?

    A. Substitution
    B. Logorrhea
    C. Echolalia
    D. Dyslogia

23. Which of the following terms refers to one's ability to discriminate between objects tactually?

    A. Proprioception
    B. Afference
    C. Stereognosis
    D. Vestibule

24. A student who has suffered a traumatic brain injury is likely to
    I. confront teachers and peers with unfair accusations
    II. act out–yelling, cursing, or other emotional outbursts
    III. be unable to adapt to changes in schedule or routine
    IV. exhibit an expressionless face

    A. I and II
    B. II, III and IV
    C. III only
    D. I, II, III and IV

25. In speech, a student often substitutes parts of words, or inappropriate words. This is known as

    A. paraphasia
    B. dysphasia
    C. nominal aphasia
    D. expressive aphasia

26. On average, which of the following consonant sounds will be mastered earliest in the speech of a child?

    A. th
    B. w
    C. s
    D. l

27. A child says, "drink" whenever she wants a drink. This is an example of

    A. logorrhea
    B. glossolalia
    C. dyslalia
    D. holophrastic speech

28. The type of hearing loss that is caused by interference with the transmission of sound from the outer ear to the inner ear is described as

    A. conductive
    B. partial
    C. mechanical
    D. sensorineural

29. Any dysfunction caused by structural deficits in the central nervous system could be described as a(n)

    A. psychogenesis
    B. organicity
    C. neurophrenia
    D. biogenesis

30. A student who is suspected of being mildly handicapped is generally assessed in the area(s) of
    I. achievement
    II. social competency
    III. intelligence
    IV. behavior

    A. I only
    B. I and III
    C. I, II, and III
    D. I, II, III and IV

31. Which of the following is a classroom observational system in which the verbal interactions between a teacher and the entire class are coded and analyzed?

    A. Fluharty
    B. Spache
    C. Flanders
    D. Montessori

32. Which of the following types of assessment is generally best for determining the most appropriate teaching objectives for a student?

    A. norm-referenced testing
    B. observation
    C. curriculum-based assessment
    D. criterion-referenced testing

33. Which of the following terms refers to a person's ability to use language in social settings?

    A. Logorrhea
    B. Lexiphasia
    C. Pragmatics
    D. Sociolalia

34. Students with vision impairments are likely to have IEP goals in the area(s) of
    I. note taking
    II. listening skills
    III. academic skill areas
    IV. mobility

    A. I, II, and IV
    B. II and III
    C. III and IV
    D. I, II, III and IV

35. Which of the following constructs, developed by Hebb, refers to that aspect of intelligence that is developed and influenced by one's environment, and that can be measured?

    A. Intelligence A
    B. Intelligence B
    C. Fluid intelligence
    D. Crystallized intelligence

36. The revised federal Individuals with Disabilities Education Act (IDEA) states that the services provided to a child with a disability must based on

    A. the child's specific educational needs
    B. the child's disability category
    C. the parents' or guardians' specific wishes
    D. the resources available at the particular educational institution

37. To safeguard a student who is having a tonic-clonic seizure, a teacher should
    I. turn the child onto his/her back
    II. attempt to revive the child
    III. place a flat, soft object under the child's head
    IV. place the child on the floor

    A. I, II and IV
    B. I, III and IV
    C. III and IV
    D. I, II, III and IV

38. In the context of special education, a "clinical type" refers to

    A. any disabling condition in which the physical features characteristic of the condition are clearly observable
    B. a method of assigning a group of students possessing a common strength or weakness a single teacher at each grade level, while the remainder of the class is heterogeneously grouped
    C. a series of disorders that are characterized by inflexible and maladaptive behavior patterns
    D. any category of disability that might impede learning

39. Which of the following sounds is considered to be a sibilant?

    A. *v*
    B. *f*
    C. *j*
    D. *th*

40. In order to maximize the communication opportunities for a student with a communication disorder, a classroom teacher should generally do each of the following, except

    A. introduce unusual or novel events
    B. provide numerous choices to the child
    C. anticipate the child's needs
    D. arrange for the child to convey information to others

41. A student's developmental quotient is derived by

    A. dividing the developmental age of any measure of development by the student's chronological age
    B. subtracting the developmental age from the chronological age
    C. dividing the chronological age by the developmental age
    D. adding the developmental age and the chronological age

42. Under the provisions of the Family Educational Rights and Privacy Act (FERPA), an educational agency or institution must notify parents of students currently in attendance of their right under the Act at least

    A. quarterly
    B. annually
    C. every two years
    D. every five years

43. Which of the following conditions will result in either an underbite or an overbite?

   A. Malocclusion
   B. Temporomandibular joint disorder (TMJ)
   C. Tonic neck reflex
   D. Maculation

44. In general, most developmentally normal children have mastered the sounds of the English language by the age of

   A. 6
   B. 8
   C. 10
   D. 12

45. What is the term used for listening, recognizing, and interpreting spoken language-at a level beyond simply hearing and responding to sounds?

   A. Auding
   B. Cohering
   C. Synthesizing
   D. Arranging

46. The label "educable mentally retarded is typically applied to those with an IQ between

   A. 0 and 25
   B. 25 and 50
   C. 50 and 75
   D. 75 and 100

47. For assessing global ability in school-age children, the most commonly used test is the

   A. Cognitive Abilities Test (CAT)
   B. Otis-Lennon Mental Ability Test (OLMAT)
   C. Kaufman Assesment Battery for Children (K-ABC)
   D. Weschler Intelligence Scale for Children (WISC)

48. Signs of juvenile rheumatoid arthritis include
   I. a tendency for stiffness to worsen during the day
   II. fever
   III. rash

   A. I only
   B. I and II
   C. II and III
   D. I, II and III

49. Of all the impairments that tend to necessitate special education services, the most prevalent is typically

   A. speech impairment
   B. learning disability
   C. mental retardation
   D. hearing impairmen

50. Norms are usually expressed in terms of each of the following, except   50._____

   A. means
   B. percentiles
   C. instructional objectives
   D. age

KEY (CORRECT ANSWERS)

1. A	11. C	21. C	31. C	41. A
2. A	12. D	22. C	32. D	42. B
3. A	13. B	23. C	33. C	43. A
4. B	14. C	24. D	34. D	44. B
5. B	15. A	25. A	35. B	45. A
6. A	16. C	26. B	36. A	46. C
7. C	17. B	27. D	37. C	47. D
8. B	18. B	28. A	38. A	48. C
9. C	19. D	29. B	39. C	49. A
10. C	20. C	30. B	40. C	50. C

EXAMINATION SECTION
TEST 1

DIRECTIONS: Each question or incomplete statement is followed by several suggested answers or completions. Select the one that BEST answers the question or completes the statement. *PRINT THE LETTER OF THE CORRECT ANSWER IN THE SPACE AT THE RIGHT.*

1. Of the following, the GREATEST problem confronting the mentally retarded adolescent is   1.____

    A. finding a job
    B. meeting the skill requirements of the job
    C. maintaining himself in the job
    D. getting a raise in pay
    E. getting a promotion in grade

2. Analyses of jobs in the food trades area reveal a variety of jobs at skill levels ranging from skilled to unskilled. One common requirement necessary for success in the food trades, regardless of skill level of the particular job, is   2.____

    A. social maturity
    B. physical stamina
    C. manual dexterity
    D. motor coordination
    E. ambition to succeed

3. The occupational-social skills in the program of occupational education are BEST taught by   3.____

    A. teaching them as a special subject
    B. integrating them within a teaching core
    C. making them the basis for every lesson
    D. reading with the children as many books as possible on the subject
    E. augmenting them with enrichment materials

4. In order to secure good group play activities in her class, the teacher should plan   4.____

    A. classroom procedures with a view to minimizing individual play activity on the part of her children
    B. group activities in which each child is chosen at least once to perform on his own
    C. to play with small groups several times before the children play without her
    D. to set aside one day a week for independent group play activity
    E. for personal participation in every group play activity which is organized

5. Parents of exceptional children are MOST likely to be   5.____

    A. mentally retarded themselves
    B. unable to accept limitations in their children
    C. uninterested in the program of occupational education
    D. too overprotective or demanding
    E. defensive about their children's limitations

6. A child from a normal progress class calls one of your special education pupils *dumb* and makes fun of him.   6.____
   In dealing with this situation, you should tell the other child that the exceptional pupil is

A. receiving special help because he is slow
B. capable of doing many, many things and is not *dumb*
C. not like other children and is, therefore, different but not *dumb*
D. now making some things that you would like to show him
E. capable of doing many things that he is not capable of doing

7. Your survey discloses that most of your pupils fail to take advantage of available neighborhood resources for constructive use of leisure time.
   Of the following, the BEST way of coping with the situation would be to

   A. undertake frequent class excursions in the neighborhood
   B. hold informal discussions about leisure-time activities in the classroom
   C. post of list of *Interesting Things To Do This Weekend* on the bulletin board
   D. write a note to parents outlining suggestions for trips
   E. find out why the available neighborhood resources are so unappealing to your pupils

8. Your survey indicates that practically none of your boys engages in reading as an out-of-school activity.
   As a FIRST step in dealing with this situation, you should

   A. insist that all the pupils in your class join the nearest branch of the public library
   B. offer a prize for the best oral book report during the week
   C. encourage the pupils to borrow books from the class library for home use
   D. build up a store of comic books to serve as a nucleus for a lending library
   E. discuss this problem with the parents and inform them of the fact that, if they do not read, their children will not read either

9. Exceptional children differ MOST from other children at school on the basis of

   A. physical appearance   B. learning ability
   C. visual-motor coordination   D. social skills
   E. experiential background

10. Exceptional pupils are MOST likely to

    A. continue to be dependent on others for economic security
    B. be institutionalized eventually
    C. be unable to make a social adjustment
    D. achieve satisfactory vocational adjustment
    E. become criminals or geniuses

11. A teacher of a group of ten-to-twelve-year-old children in a special education class has formulated several projects in the development of social skills. The training in these skills is

    A. *advisable* because of their importance in every phase of the pupils' present and future life
    B. *advisable* because they are required for success on the job
    C. *inadvisable* because such projects cannot be taught formally to a special education group

D. *inadvisable* because such projects are best learned through out-of-school experiences
E. *inadvisable* because these projects will only serve to re-emphasize the fact that exceptional children are different from other children

12. In developing an intercultural education program for a class of twelve-to-fourteen-year-old pupils, the BEST aim for the teacher would be to

    A. give her pupils an understanding of the religions represented in her class
    B. demonstrate the fact that all races have inadequacies
    C. give her pupils an appreciation of the cultural contributions of the racial groups represented in her class
    D. show her pupils the inadequacies of the doctrine of racial superiority
    E. show the need for respect for people as individuals

13. The interdependence of the members of the present-day society can BEST be taught to a group of ten-year-old pupils through

    A. an understanding of the functions of the workers in their local community
    B. a unit on the United Nations
    C. an understanding of the *One World* concept
    D. lessons on the importance of the city's manufactures to the farmers of America
    E. a unit demonstrating that a group of students work more efficiently than one student alone

14. The physical and social maturity of the mentally retarded child is USUALLY _____ his academic achievement.

    A. at the same level as   B. above
    C. slightly below   D. far below
    E. far above

15. You observe that one of your more able pupils is withdrawn and does not participate spontaneously in the activities of the class.
    You should

    A. call upon him to recite frequently before the class in order to make the group conscious of his presence
    B. tell him that he must take a greater part in the activities of the class or you will stop calling on him
    C. indicate that he can make friends more readily by being more generous with his candy
    D. develop group situations in which he is gradually led to participate with his classmates
    E. call him aside and probe the reasons why he does not participate more

16. A sociogram would MOST likely be used for the study of

    A. differential preferences for the various curricular areas
    B. attitudes toward the school
    C. most and least popular children
    D. attitudes toward the teacher
    E. principles of group formation

17. Which of the following statements is INCORRECT as a guide for the development of anecdotal records by the teacher?

    A. Observation and recording should be systematic.
    B. Inferences and interpretations should be recorded rather than mere facts.
    C. Anecdotes should be concrete and concise.
    D. Periodic review, diagnosis, and interpretation should be made.
    E. Anecdotal records should be objective rather than diagnostic and prognostic.

18. Education for the mentally retarded consists of a fivefold program: Occupational Information, Vocational Guidance, Vocational Training, Vocational Placement, and Social Placement.
    For which of these five phases is the special education classroom teacher responsible?
    All

    A. five phases
    B. but vocational placement
    C. but social placement
    D. but vocational and social placement
    E. but vocational training

19. The mentally retarded child is MOST likely to be happy and to succeed in the type of job in which

    A. little or no direct teaching of the skills involved is required
    B. the work is essentially repetitive in character, as in assembly line jobs
    C. the work is done in small, supervised groups and involves some change in operation
    D. little more than physical strength is required
    E. a challenge is consistently presented in the form of principles and concepts to be mastered

20. A parent in a low-income family comes to school to inquire as to why her otherwise normal child is not reading up to grade level.
    The MOST appropriate among the following comments which might be made by the child's teacher to the parent is:

    A. We have this problem with many low-income children.
    B. Considering everything, your child is doing as well as expected.
    C. Your child is handicapped by the lack of books in the home.
    D. The chances are that your child is capable of doing better in reading than at present.
    E. Parents are often used by their children as models; thus, it seems that if you read more, your child will be encouraged to do likewise.

21. All of the following statements are correct EXCEPT that proponents of homogeneous grouping

    A. call heterogeneous grouping undemocratic
    B. claim that heterogeneous grouping deters the academic achievement of brighter pupils

C. state that slower children obtain a worse image of themselves under heterogeneous grouping
D. insist that teachers find heterogeneous grouping to be unmanageable for instructional purposes
E. agree that the problem of individual differences is minimized when students are grouped homogeneously

22. The opposite of the *melting pot* theory in assessing the role of immigrants in the United States is the theory of

    A. acculturation
    B. cultural pluralism
    C. assimilation
    D. desegregation
    E. integration

23. Of the following statements, the one which is CORRECT in regard to the teaching of English to Puerto Rican pupils is that

    A. emphasis should be placed upon creating an English-speaking atmosphere with pupils being forbidden to speak Spanish in the classroom
    B. the teacher should be fluent in Spanish
    C. Spanish may occasionally be employed to check pupil comprehension of English
    D. new words should be taught through pictures first, then through objects
    E. the repetition of phrases and idioms has been found to be one of the most effective methods

24. Of the following approaches to the use of a sociogram, the one which is LEAST effective is that in which the teacher tells the children

    A. that their choices will be held confidential
    B. to make a first, second, and third selection
    C. that they should try to be as honest as they can in making their choices
    D. that they may include absentees among their choices
    E. to write the names of those they would not like as friends, as well as friends they have chosen

25. Of the following, the MOST important educational value of taking children on trips to art museums is to

    A. help them relate art objects to the lives of people in various times
    B. teach them how to act in public
    C. help them learn the names of many artists
    D. give them some ideas to copy
    E. instill in them an understanding and an appreciation of painting and sculpture

26. When a parent expresses the fear that her child's education will suffer because there are several minority group children in the child's class, the BEST *convincer* that the child's education will not suffer is to

    A. invite her to visit your classroom to observe the children of the class at work
    B. inform her that each child must learn to live and play with children of all groups
    C. discuss with the parent the background of the minority group children
    D. display the work which the children of the class have completed
    E. refer the parent to several educational and psychological references which support heterogeneous grouping

27. It is an acknowledged fact that no class can be homogeneous with respect to a plurality of abilities. The pragmatic consequences for class instruction are that

    A. patterns of grouping should vary in accordance with the particular aims and purposes that are being served at the time
    B. with each change of activity there should be a regrouping of pupils
    C. workbook activity should accompany each academic lesson
    D. the teacher should teach the class as one group, gearing her instruction to the middle of the class
    E. each child should be expected to make at least one contribution in each lesson or activity

28. Of the following objectives of having children work in committees, the MOST important is to

    A. develop self-direction in the areas of the social amenities and of parliamentary procedure
    B. improve children's ability in speaking effectively before a group
    C. develop initiative and leadership qualities of the bright children and encourage the shy children
    D. make learning a cooperative enterprise in thinking through and solving problems
    E. stimulate competition within and between groups which will serve to promote greater interest in the group activity

29. Of the following, the LEAST effective way to guide the development of proper attitudes in the social studies is to

    A. plan a series of appropriate experiences
    B. manifest positive teacher attitudes to pupils and parents
    C. provide individual and group guidance techniques
    D. have pupils memorize and discuss a set of significant statements
    E. permit or encourage pupil planning or pupil chairing of the unit

30. Of the following situations used to motivate children, the one which MOST NEARLY exemplifies intrinsic motivation is that in which pupils

    A. strive to maintain good attendance because the class will be awarded a banner
    B. behave well because they are *reported* if they do not
    C. are concerned with correctness of writing because they are publishing a class newspaper
    D. work hard because they wish to be placed on the Honor Roll
    E. organize committees to study distant lands because of an assignment by their teacher

31. When a teacher helps a pupil to convert socially unacceptable impulses into socially approved actions, she is helping him to use the technique of

    A. sublimation B. compensation C. rationalization
    D. projection   E. introspection

32. In helping children to learn how to accept and fulfill responsibilities, the teacher may properly permit them to make decisions with respect to all of the following questions EXCEPT:

    A. What exits shall we use during fire drills?
    B. How can every child have a chance to paint?
    C. Where shall our science center be located?
    D. How can we use our spelling test results to help us improve?
    E. How should we organize our desks for the reading hour?

33. In his book, THE EDUCATION OF AMERICAN TEACHERS, James B. Conant put forward all of the following ideas EXCEPT that

    A. education courses should be downgraded in importance
    B. more stress should be put on practice teaching
    C. teacher-training institutions should have no responsibility for teacher certification
    D. the emphasis in appraising new teachers should be shifted to observation of classroom performance
    E. an internship period for teachers should be provided

34. Jose, a bilingual child from Puerto Rico, has just entered a class composed exclusively of mainland children. Of the following procedures calculated to create acceptance of Jose by his peers, the MOST effective one is for the teacher to

    A. make Jose's *expert* knowledge available to a committee working on *Daily Life in Latin America*
    B. learn some Spanish phrases and teach them to the class to make Jose feel at home
    C. place books on Puerto Rico in the class library so that other pupils can learn to understand Jose better
    D. create desirable attitudes toward Jose by having the class discuss the need for tolerance
    E. develop special group situations in which Jose's fluency in Spanish will make him stand out

35. A teacher set up a classroom student court so that when a child disobeyed a class rule, the children themselves would decide what the offender's punishment should be. This situation is fundamentally

    A. *good* because the wrongdoer is being judged by his peers
    B. *bad* because the emphasis is on punishment rather than on a positive reconstruction of the child's behavior
    C. *good* because children tend to have greater insight in such situations and their punishment is likely to be more fitting than that proposed by the teacher
    D. *bad* because the teacher may have to impose a more severe punishment if the children let the offender off too lightly
    E. *good* because a student court is probably a better deterrent of student *crimes* than teacher punishment

36. Of the following statements about the *Individualized Reading Program,* the one that is NOT true is that

   A. the child may choose reading materials according to his interests and desires
   B. reading is not thought of in terms of categories such as *instructional reading, outside reading,* etc.
   C. the plan requires individual conferences between teacher and pupil
   D. phonics is one of the methods used
   E. teachers no longer have to teach lessons in the basic reading skills

37. Among the following, the MOST reasonable approach in dealing with correct usage in the elementary school is to

   A. demand correct English from all children at all times
   B. set up a list of correct usages for each grade and require each child to show mastery of the grade requirement
   C. list each child's errors and have him write corrective exercises for homework
   D. draw up a list of correct and incorrect usage and assign a few examples of each for homework every day
   E. let the children engage in many activities in which acceptable usage will be heard, read, spoken, and written

38. The statement which is NOT generally true about choral speaking is that

   A. the timid child tends to lose his self-consciousness and to participate readily
   B. the individual child must learn to suppress individual conceptions or interpretations
   C. children tend to let their choral speaking become *singsong*
   D. children often strive for loudness, thus producing a strained or forced type of tone
   E. children who cannot carry a tune do not appreciably hinder the group

39. Among the following, an attitude of cooperation is LEAST likely to be fostered by

   A. giving reasons why helpfulness is a good way of life
   B. providing opportunities for experiencing pleasure in helping other children
   C. setting a proper example
   D. providing opportunities for accomplishing things with other children
   E. showing approval each time the child makes a worthwhile contribution

40. Education in the United States is usually looked upon as a *state function* because

   A. the United States Constitution specifically grants authority over education to the states
   B. the Supreme Court has held that the United States government may pass no law about education
   C. President Washington decided that the federal government would not support schools
   D. the Supreme Court has held that, barring unusual circumstances, laws dealing with education are delegated to the states
   E. the United States Constitution does not mention education

41. If a teacher asks each pupil in her class to write the name of the classmate whom he would like most to have on his committee, she is MOST likely gathering data for a(n)

    A. interest inventory
    B. sociogram
    C. case study
    D. personality scale
    E. class party

42. All of the following statements are generally true of children of elementary school age EXCEPT:
    Girls

    A. mature approximately one year earlier than do boys
    B. have poorer health than boys
    C. excel in body balance and fine hand coordination
    D. excel in school achievement
    E. tend to get their second set of teeth earlier than boys

43. Of the following ways of setting up committees in social studies, the one MOST likely to result in effective committee work is to

    A. have committees formed on a purely voluntary basis
    B. have the teacher select the chairmen and committee members
    C. have the teacher assign chairmen who will select their committees
    D. form committees under the teacher's guidance after teacher-pupil planning
    E. administer a sociometric test and, based on the results obtained, divide the class into the appropriate committees

44. All of the following statements are consistent with the educational philosophy of John Dewey EXCEPT:

    A. Education must be conceived as a continuing reconstruction of experience
    B. The process and the goal of education are one and the same thing
    C. Moral discipline should be a part and outcome of school life, not something proceeding from the teacher
    D. Students should engage in school and classroom activities that have a functional value
    E. The acquisition of subject matter by children remains the basic task of the school

45. A newly arrived Salvadoran child who speaks English haltingly enters a teacher's class.
    Of the following, the procedure which is LAST in order of priority is to

    A. increase the child's English vocabulary so that he may function better
    B. provide useful experiences which will help the child to adjust more readily to mainland life
    C. determine the health and nutritional needs of the child
    D. involve him in class activities so that he may become a functioning member of the class
    E. eliminate the foreign accent from the child's speech so that he will bear no stigma in his relations with his peers

46. It is reliably reported to a teacher that many members of her class have engaged in petty vandalism on the school grounds.
Of the following, the MOST effective way for her to handle the problem is to

   A. have a class art contest for the purpose of providing decorations to beautify the room
   B. have the pupils engage in creative writing during a language arts lesson on *Avoiding Temptation To Do What is Wrong*
   C. do direct teaching, as part of the social studies program, on the importance of respect for public property
   D. have a meeting of the children's mothers and discuss the problem
   E. analyze the possible reasons why the class acted in such a socially unacceptable manner

46.____

47. All of the following authors are known for their writings on child development EXCEPT

   A. Milly Almy
   B. Benjamin Spock
   C. Arnold Gesell
   D. Gunnar Myrdal
   E. Arthur Jersild

47.____

48. *We conclude that in the field of public education the doctrine of "separate but equal" has no place* were the words used by Chief Justice

   A. Robert B. Taney
   B. Charles E. Hughes
   C. Earl Warren
   D. John Marshall
   E. William H. Taft

48.____

49. The teacher of a sixth grade class is likely to find all of the following characteristics among children of this growth level EXCEPT that they

   A. are influenced very little by what their peers do
   B. are beginning to rebel against adult domination
   C. are at a receptive stage for indoctrination of all sorts
   D. enjoy giving assistance to younger children in the lower grades
   E. are beginning to show more discrimination in the selection of possessions and in the care of them

49.____

50. Of the following, the BEST way for a teacher to help children who are inexperienced in committee work is to

   A. work with a group composed of superior pupils
   B. train one committee while the rest of the class observes
   C. guide the work of one committee while the rest of the class is engaged in other activities
   D. discuss working space and materials for each committee
   E. work with a group composed of slow learners

50.____

KEY (CORRECT ANSWERS)

1. C	11. A	21. A	31. A	41. B
2. A	12. E	22. B	32. A	42. B
3. B	13. A	23. C	33. C	43. D
4. E	14. B	24. E	34. A	44. E
5. D	15. D	25. A	35. B	45. E
6. C	16. C	26. A	36. E	46. C
7. A	17. B	27. A	37. E	47. D
8. C	18. D	28. D	38. B	48. C
9. B	19. C	29. D	39. A	49. A
10. A	20. D	30. C	40. E	50. B

EXAMINATION SECTION
TEST 1

DIRECTIONS: Each question or incomplete statement is followed by several suggested answers or completions. Select the one that BEST answers the question or completes the statement. *PRINT THE LETTER OF THE CORRECT ANSWER IN THE SPACE AT THE RIGHT.*

1. During the past twenty years, there has been considerable research to determine the effectiveness of communication nets in small groups. Two of the simplest of the nets are:

   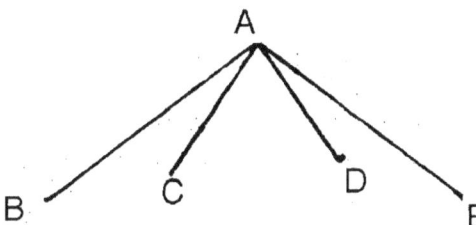 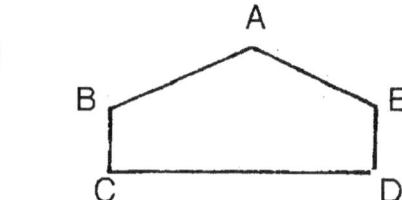

   In each of these, the letter represents an individual and the line a means of two-way communication. The findings, to date, have tended to support the view that the use of Network I rather than Network II will result in

   A. less enthusiasm among the participants
   B. slower action in solving problems
   C. higher morale in the group as a whole
   D. greater adaptability to change
   E. less flexibility in making administrative decisions

   1.____

2. For group work to be MOST effective in the teaching of reading in a fourth grade class, the groups should consist of pupils who are chosen in terms of their being similar in

   A. emotional age   B. intelligence quotient
   C. mental age   D. reading age
   E. chronological age

   2.____

3. The sociogram is a helpful means of enabling a guidance counselor and the staff to determine the

   A. interrelationships among the pupils in a class
   B. social agencies to which they can turn for assistance in solving behavior and personality problems
   C. social conditions in the school neighborhood
   D. family relationships which are causative factors in personality maladjustment
   E. social maturity of a given group

   3.____

4. Indicate the MOST correct statement: Anecdotal records should

   A. set forth the teacher's personal reactions to the children
   B. stress accounts of misbehavior
   C. present an objective picture of the child's reactions
   D. constitute a major means to wholesome adjustment
   E. emphasize the teacher's recommendations

   4.____

5. The MOST important factor conducive to successful group work

   A. is initiative and self-direction on the part of the pupil
   B. is effective classroom management on the part of the teacher
   C. requires that necessary materials be placed within easy reach of the pupils
   D. requires that memoranda to show the sequence of activities to be followed by different groups be written on the blackboard
   E. is effective classroom management by a class-elected leader

6. In most cases, groups should

   A. be based on the abilities of the pupils
   B. be based on the interests, abilities, and achievements of the pupils
   C. consist of the same pupils for all curriculum areas
   D. be based primarily on the physical limitations of the children
   E. be based on the results of sociometric tests

7. The BEST illustration of pupil participation in a social situation in mathematics is found where

   A. each pupil has an opportunity in a *store situation* to be either storekeeper or customer, whichever he prefers
   B. the teacher acts as storekeeper and asks the pupils to solve a given problem
   C. one pupil acts as the teacher and calls on the pupils to work store problems at the blackboard
   D. each pupil finds the total cost of two or more articles in the store by counting paper money at his desk
   E. each pupil has an opportunity in a *store situation,* at one time or another, to be storekeeper and customer

8. If group work is to be effective,

   A. there must be more than three groups
   B. the children must receive training in responsibility for their own activities
   C. group duties should not be rotated for long periods of time
   D. the teacher should always select the groups
   E. the groups must be stable and homogeneous

9. The teacher can BEST study the pupil-pupil relationships in her class by using one of the following techniques:

   A. anecdotal records   B. sociogram
   C. three wishes   D. dramatic play
   E. cumulative record

10. The aim of the so-called *progressive education* may BEST be expressed as

    A. development of the social group
    B. tolerant understanding and creative self-expression
    C. development of leadership
    D. training in necessary skills
    E. the integration of education with political action

11. Deficient mentality is the cause of juvenile delinquency   11._____

    A. to a very great degree   B. in the majority of cases
    C. in almost 50 percent of cases   D. to a slight degree
    E. invariably

12. School groupings should be   12._____

    A. fluid
    B. heterogeneous
    C. strictly homogeneous
    D. more heterogeneous than homogeneous
    E. avoided

13. Of the following, the SOUNDEST basis for moral growth is   13._____

    A. desire for approbation
    B. desire to achieve a good reputation
    C. respect for authority
    D. sense of duty
    E. recognition of the rights of man

14. The prime essential of all good management is the elimination of waste.   14._____
    In school, the GREATEST wastes as well as the greatest values are in

    A. matters of organization
    B. mechanization of routine
    C. teaching and study
    D. care of textbooks and school equipment and efficient use of the school plant
    E. the public information system

15. The approach MOST commonly used by the teacher for evaluating personal-social   15._____
    adjustment is

    A. a personality inventory   B. the anecdotal record
    C. observation   D. an interview
    E. the sociogram

16. Of the following, the one which the teacher of a class can evaluate MOST objectively is   16._____

    A. personality growth
    B. what the previous teacher of the child has done
    C. achievement in academic subjects
    D. feeling of security and personal worth
    E. rate of learning

17. Of the following, the MOST potent force that can be utilized to change the behavior of an   17._____
    adolescent is disapproval of the behavior voiced by

    A. his parents   B. the teacher of his class
    C. a group of his peers   D. a teacher he admires
    E. a policeman

18. For the most part, the MAJOR concerns of adolescents center about

   A. personal status
   B. good health
   C. beauty
   D. money
   E. physical appearance

19. The following are three examples of anecdotal records which have been written by teachers:
   I. John is continually taking things that belong to other boys in the class. He is the biggest sneak-thief I have ever taught.
   II. This morning John started a fight with Elaine when my back was turned. You have to watch him every minute or he gets into trouble.
   III. When called on this morning, John gave an excellent answer to a difficult question. He has yet to volunteer any information in class.

   If the above behavior descriptions were arranged in order of their adequacy, from best to poorest, the CORRECT sequence would be

   A. III, II, I
   B. III, I, II
   C. II, III, I
   D. II, I, III
   E. I, II, III

20. In a program of arts and crafts for the physically handicapped,

   A. the quality of workmanship is unimportant
   B. the aim is to teach leisure time activities
   C. the goals of achievement are the same as for normal children
   D. the goals of achievement need not be set within the child's limitations
   E. adjustments must be made in consideration of the child's disabilities

21. Which one of the following concepts in teaching English to Puerto Rican children is CORRECT?

   A. Repetition is not effective in teaching the new language.
   B. Translation of Spanish by the teacher is acceptable.
   C. The basic vocabulary should be predicated on the new situation.
   D. Begin with written forms of commonplace objects.
   E. Make the change to English as swift and complete as possible.

22. According to some investigators, the parents of school-age cerebral palsied children were found to be more concerned about their children's mental and educational potentialities than about their physical defects. Which one of the following is CORRECT?

   A. Parents of cerebral palsied children are justified in this emphasis because they feel there is little they can do about the child's body.
   B. This reflects an attitude of overindulgence and overprotection on the part of the parent.
   C. Parents are prone to try to compensate for the physical disability of such children by forcing them to intellectual attainments and achievements.
   D. This parental attitude is in accord with the view that it is better for the child to focus on his assets and play down his limitations.
   E. These parents are aware of the fact that although cerebral palsied children are physically handicapped, a large majority of them have superior intellectual capacities.

23. In order to lead the child to gain a better understanding of how people live in distant lands, the teacher should   23._____

    A. put emphasis on geographical facts and relationships
    B. emphasize the strange and the quaint
    C. stress the dramatic customs
    D. bring out the basic similarities among peoples
    E. bring out the basic differences among peoples

24. The central focus of the arts and crafts experience for physically handicapped children should be   24._____

    A. development of technical skill
    B. making gifts for others to enjoy
    C. learning to handle new materials
    D. giving personal expression through an art medium
    E. exposing the children to a new leisure-time activity

25. A homebound teacher has been asked by the parents of a student with hemophilia to help the boy develop cultural interests that are physically appropriate for him. Which of the following procedures would be LEAST appropriate for this teacher to follow?   25._____

    A. Arrange a group meeting at the boy's home of several other homebound students, each of whom has prepared a short talk on a cultural activity that he has found pleasurable.
    B. Administer an interest inventory test to the student that will provide a starting point for discussion of possible cultural pursuits.
    C. Discuss with the parents the kind of activities they would like the boy to follow, based upon their observation of his habits.
    D. Based on the interests and aptitudes the boy has already shown in his work, discuss with him extensions that will eventually be culturally enriching.
    E. Discuss with the boy the kind of activities other homebound students have found enjoyable and present the possibility of his choosing one or more of these activities.

26. Interest in manual skills, in handcrafts, and in hobbies among homebound students is emphasized because   26._____

    A. future occupational and vocational opportunities often develop from these sources
    B. such activities are normal and necessary in the development of all children
    C. they provide quiet occupation for children whose physical activities are seriously restricted
    D. handicapped children usually develop compensatory skills in those areas
    E. these children cannot concentrate on their regular work assignments for long periods of time

27. Positive civic attitudes can BEST be developed in children by

    A. citing widely accepted moral precepts
    B. discussing the necessity for good attitudes in a series of lessons
    C. preparing a good citizenship chart for each child to keep and mark himself
    D. discussing the values and merits of good citizenship
    E. guiding their conduct in daily activities

28. To promote growth in social responsibility on the part of the exceptional child, the teacher should

    A. help the children develop a code of behavior
    B. set up a *Court of Justice* to punish the pupils who violate class rules
    C. provide opportunities where they may utilize social approval or disapproval
    D. organize a systematic series of lessons on the social responsibilities of citizens
    E. take the class on a trip to the local courts

29. A chronological account kept by a teacher of a child's day actions and adjustment in various school settings is a report which is BEST termed

    A. psychological   B. sociometric   C. biographical
    D. cumulative   E. anecdotal

30. The social attitudes of adolescent children in special education classes, when compared with those of other children, are

    A. less susceptible to influence by peer groups
    B. more susceptible to influence by peer groups
    C. influenced to about the same degree by peer groups
    D. more rigid and less spontaneous
    E. more susceptible to influence by teachers and parents

31. In a special education class, the MOST important area to teach is

    A. social living   B. language arts
    C. practical arts   D. social studies
    E. basic information

32. During adolescence, the attitudes of children enrolled in special education classes are

    A. strongly influenced by the group with which they associate
    B. strongly influenced by authoritarian adults
    C. relatively more crystallized than those of normal children
    D. more stable than those of more intelligent children
    E. more strongly influenced by respected adults than by the group with which they may associate

33. A successful adaptation by an exceptional child to the social-cultural world depends on

    A. his intelligence
    B. his acceptance of himself as inferior
    C. his knowing his place among superiors
    D. the attitudes of society toward him
    E. his ability to adapt to new situations

34. Studies of retarded children transferred to more favorable social, emotional, and economic environments have demonstrated

    A. the constancy of the I.Q.
    B. that environmental changes significantly affect the I.Q.
    C. that heredity is more important than environment in determining intellectual level
    D. that environment is more important than heredity in determining the I.Q.
    E. that environmental changes affect emotional development to a greater extent than they do intellectual development

35. A progress chart for mentally retarded children should show each child competing with

    A. all the other children in the class
    B. his own record
    C. the children of his group
    D. all children with the same MA
    E. all children with the same or similar I.Q.

36. A teacher of a special education class must recognize that specific skills

    A. must be taught apart from other learnings in order to be most effective
    B. can rarely be integrated with the curricular core
    C. are to be tied into the core experience
    D. are to be taught on occasion as the situation calls for them
    E. must be emphasized more than the core experience

37. The PRIMARY aim of the occupational education program for low I.Q. children is to

    A. give them beginning techniques in reading
    B. provide enjoyable activities
    C. train them in simple manual skills
    D. give them a head start in developing their skills
    E. develop desirable social habits

38. Generally speaking, the mentally retarded child who needs LEAST help in securing employment is the

    A. unskilled helper   B. semi-skilled worker
    C. sheltered helper   D. sheltered worker
    E. ambitious applicant

39. A study found that changes of residence for subnormal adults as compared with normal adults were

    A. more frequent both within and out of a neighborhood
    B. less frequent both within and out of a neighborhood
    C. more frequent in toto, but less frequent within a neighborhood
    D. less frequent in toto, but more frequent within a neighborhood
    E. more frequent within a neighborhood, less frequent without a neighborhood, and more frequent in toto

40. The exceptional child reacts to the classroom situation in terms of his

    A. intelligence   B. home background
    C. social development   D. past experience
    E. perceptive ability

41. Mary, a ten-year-old in your class, bids for your attention all the time. 41._____
    The BEST means for handling this situation is to

    A. ignore her
    B. give her all the attention she craves
    C. notice her only when she needs you most
    D. provide satisfying social relationships with the other children
    E. notify the guidance counselor and present your observations to him

42. The results of a test administered to a child by a psychologist from the Bureau of Child 42._____
    Guidance shows that he has an I.Q. of approximately 75.
    The placement of this child in a special education class should depend upon the

    A. parents' consent
    B. teacher's recommendation
    C. psychologist's test results
    D. child's consent
    E. results of a conference between the psychologist, the parent, and the principal

43. Curriculum adjustment for mentally retarded children is GENERALLY characterized by 43._____

    A. one-the-job training of the late adolescent
    B. emphasis on training for citizenship at the adolescent level
    C. postponement of vocational skills until the junior high school level
    D. emphasis on manual skills after the primary level
    E. a trial-and-error sequence

44. Instruction on the narcotics problem in classes of adolescent retardates in large cities 44._____
    USUALLY

    A. should be given by the school doctor or nurse
    B. is left to the discretion of the individual teacher
    C. should depend upon the prevalence of addiction in the area in which the school is
       located
    D. is mandated by state law
    E. is mandated by local ordinance

45. For satisfactory functioning in the community, the following minimum reading level is 45._____
    GENERALLY necessary in the _____ year.

    A. third   B. fourth   C. fifth
    D. sixth   E. seventh

46. Vocational guidance of non-academic children should 46._____

    A. enable the child to realize his own capabilities and limitations
    B. introduce the child to a broad program of reading material giving occupational
       information
    C. advise the child realistically of his unfitness for unsuitable job area in which he may
       be interested
    D. deal chiefly with vocational areas which interest the majority of the class
    E. lead the child to choose any unskilled type job

47. On the adolescent level, the program of occupational information developed for special education pupils aims to

    A. concentrate interest on the types of semi-skilled jobs currently available in the community
    B. center around job areas which have teenage appeal
    C. give the pupil an understanding of the requirements of many kinds of jobs - unskilled, semi-skilled, and skilled
    D. encourage the pupil to select for intensive study one or two jobs for which he is best fitted
    E. inform the pupil of the types of unskilled, semiskilled, and skilled jobs which he will be qualified to fill when he leaves school

48. In planning language work for older adolescents, the teacher of a special education class should consider that

    A. oral communication should receive more emphasis than written expression
    B. less emphasis should be placed on oral than on written expression
    C. equal emphasis should be placed on both oral and written expression
    D. the exceptional pupil generally attains sixth-year language ability
    E. the exceptional pupil should be trained in social poise and expression

49. The summary of the psychological examination given by the Bureau of Child Guidance is marked *Personal and Confidential*. Assume that the Bureau is concerned about a case that has reached the social agencies, the school, and the courts.
    The information contained in this report should NOT be divulged to

    A. case workers representing social agencies
    B. the principal and guidance counselors
    C. the affected teachers in the school
    D. probation officers affiliated with a municipal court
    E. psychologists engaged in private practice

50. Mentally retarded children learn social skills BEST by

    A. association   B. incidental teaching
    C. imitation   D. demonstration
    E. direct teaching

KEY (CORRECT ANSWERS)

1. A	11. D	21. C	31. A	41. D
2. D	12. A	22. C	32. A	42. E
3. A	13. D	23. D	33. D	43. B
4. C	14. C	24. D	34. B	44. E
5. B	15. C	25. C	35. B	45. B
6. B	16. C	26. B	36. C	46. A
7. E	17. C	27. E	37. E	47. C
8. B	18. A	28. C	38. C	48. A
9. B	19. A	29. D	39. D	49. B
10. A	20. E	30. C	40. D	50. E

www.ingramcontent.com/pod-product-compliance
Lightning Source LLC
Chambersburg PA
CBHW081823300426
44116CB00014B/2466